The Detox

Chef Tawah Lightfoot EL

Contents

Nutrition & Metabolism   39

Success Stories

The members of the 30-day detox program with Chef Lightfoot El were asked to share their experiences.

This is what they had to say

"Overall, it was a beautiful experience for me. This was something I've always wanted to do, but I did not know how. The support system was amazing. I did not have a set weight that I wanted to lose. I simply wanted to get off these bloody meds. I wanted to feel like I was living. I did not want to live with pain in my body. Thirteen long years of being on meds. . I was willing to try anything. I stayed hungry in the beginning, but I got stronger as time progressed. The level of knowledge I've gained is priceless. I am honored. You are a great teacher. Your wealth of knowledge is out of this world."

- Albertha Elritha Hewitt

Acknowledgements

- Mrs Greene
- Mr Greene
- Elizabeth Bursey
- Carry Rose
- Azima Lightfoot El
- Kayden B
- Tasha B
- Danridge H
- Deon H
- Devon H
- Dian P
- Stephanie P
- At-sik-hata Nation Of Yamassee Moors
- Eric Blanks
- Anita Wright
- Takitta Ollison
- Assata Azingha
- Dextrel Covington
- O.G Wiz
- David Rodriguez
- Michael Lambe
- Professor Ogonna A'bolu
- Brandon Ballestero
- Shirley Wu

"30-day liquid fast. Finally finished. Feeling brand new minus 50 lbs."

- Dwayne Corprew

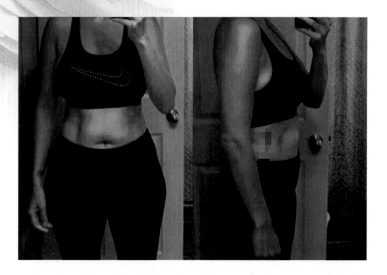

"Overall a great experience. The class was well managed, explained and monitored.

Now that I am done with the fast and eating again, I have noticed my bowel movements are very regular and not smelly! I have very little desire to eat the junk presented at the office. (Today someone brought in ribs.) What would have smelled yum to me a few months ago smelled pretty rancid and greasy. So happy I reset my health."

- Kel

"I enjoyed learning this level of discipline. I had never done this before, and didn't think I could. After day 5, it became easier. I realized that my body is as strong as my mind allows. I am also happy with the results of the detox, weight loss and renewal. Thanks for the tough love Chef Lightfoot El."

- Laquita A. Humphrey

FOR MORE COMPREHENSIVE & EXCITING
STORIES, PLEASE CHECK THE LAST PAGES
OF THIS BOOK.

ABDUR KULL SHAAYUAAT BI WAH SAAMUS SHIL PA TEMP TA

BEGIN ALL THINGS BY FIRST USING THE ALL

Introduction

There's so much misinformation out there about how to live a healthy lifestyle when it comes to nutrition. When it comes to cultivating a good eating and drinking habit, people are always being told what they should and should not eat without having the slightest clue about why. People will perform a detox and go on a detox diet, buy various detox supplements or join a detox program without a proper understanding of how our bodies work, the nature and origin of toxins our bodies are exposed to, and how nutrition comes into the picture.

This book provides valuable insight on nutrition, the vital organs responsible for getting rid of toxins, the function of these organs and virtually everything you need to know about toxins in a way that's easy to understand without the technical, medical jargon.

- Chef Lightfoot El

DETOXIFICATION, the New BUZZWORD

A lot of people are unhappy. They want to know the solutions to their problems. They want people to tell them they have a problem. Why? It's easy to become a victim. Welcome to the health industry. It's a lovely place where everybody seems to have a problem or develop one. The ones who claim to have the cure end up taking your hard-earned money by giving you a "solution". After the exchange of money for this "solution," you'll get to live happily after. Right? I wish life was that easy. While some genuine ones are knowledgeable with a lot of experience dealing with health issues, a lot of the so-called "special ones" are just snake oil salesmen that would make you believe you have a problem when you don't or take advantage of the fact that you truly have a problem to add a few bucks to their pockets.

In the health industry, there are always discoveries about a particular type of plant, chemical substance or nutrient that would solve all your health problems if you can lay your hands on them. While there are some particular discoveries or research that tend to enlighten the masses on certain things, the snake oil salesmen see it as an opportunity to create more problems. They use the popularity of the discovery, create a significant problem that the said discovery would help to treat, and then ask us to pay for the solution. Funny enough, we can't wait to pay for this solution even if we don't understand the problem we supposedly have or how the solution even works. We have a problem and we have someone with the solution. So, why should we take the time to think? We pay for the said solution and then discover whether it did or didn't work for our non-existent problem. Another option is for the said solution to work due to the medical community term, "the placebo effect".

Detoxification, detoxing, and detox are the new hot topics in the health industry. Everybody is telling you to detox. Your body needs to go through detoxification for your lost beauty to come back. You need to detox for your body to lose weight and so on. Everyone can't wait to sell you their magical pills, diets or programs that would make your body get rid of toxins, lose weight, be void of diseases, gain strength and so on.

How many of these claims are true? Do the proposed solutions work? If they do work, what exactly do they do? Is there an iota of truth in all these? Where does reality meet Disney? For you to know all these, you need to get to the root and find your way up. The root being the word – *detoxification*.

Detoxification

Detoxification (noun) is a word derived from the word *detoxify* (verb). According to medicinenet.com, the word *detoxify* means: *To reduce or eliminate the toxicity of a substance or poison. To promote the recovery of a person from an addictive drug such as alcohol or heroin.* When you take the word and understand it from the angle of detoxifying your body, it holds appeal. We all can't wait to get rid of some toxins from our bodies. What's more? Our bodies actually go through detoxification!

So where do the toxins come from?

The toxins or toxicants (as you will learn in the next chapters) can be found everywhere; in our homes, offices, environment, the air we breathe, the water we drink, the objects we use every day and so on.

Our bodies also produce toxins as a result of metabolic processes during our bodily functions. The pile-up of toxins in our bodies could lead to a lot of health issues. Hence, the need for detoxification to avoid putting too much strain on our organs, especially those responsible for carrying out the detoxification in our body.

Now, this is where it gets interesting. Our bodies are fully capable of carrying out the process of detoxification without the need for a pill or any other type of aide. Our bodies have successfully done this process since creation.

So what exactly does the claim of detoxifying our body and getting rid of toxins entail? In most cases, to help our organs perform their job efficiently.

If our bodies are fully capable of carrying out the function of detoxifying, do we truly need the "extra help" peddle?

Here is the catch, while our bodies are fully capable of detoxifying and getting rid of toxins from our bodies, it is usually under a lot of added strain caused by our eating and drinking habits, health and lifestyle choices, the environment and so on. All these could lead to our organs not working to full capacity or being overwhelmed by too many toxins. Not good at all.

In this book, you will learn more about toxins, what detoxification entails, what goes on in our bodies during detoxification, the organs responsible for detoxification, how our eating habits and activities affect detoxification, how to help our bodies in the detoxification process and much more. Included in this book is an actionable 30-day detox program you can use to help you start your detoxing process.

While our detoxifying organs and systems are up to the task of eliminating toxins, the constant exposure to environmental toxins combined with unhealthy eating habits have tipped the balance in favor of toxins. Our organs are not performing up to the level in which they were designed. Our health and wellness are suffering for it. The facts are around us. The increase in obesity, decrease in productivity, and the increase in health issues such as serious headaches, fatigue, sleeping disorders, anxiety, cardiovascular disease, high blood pressure, diabetes, cancer, etc. all point to the problem.

Right now, we need to tip the balance back to favor our bodies by helping our organs that are in charge of neutralizing the effect and flushing of the toxins from our body. You can call it a sort of fortification or reinforcement. To do this, we need to take a step back and have a proper rethink on how we can motivate our organs to help us.

As Will Mcavoy once said, "The first step in solving a problem is recognizing there is one." The same thing applies here. For you to be able to tip the balance back in your favor, you need to acknowledge and accept you have a problem. Only when you accept you have a problem, can your body and mind work together in harmony on embarking on whatever it takes to correct or solve the problem.

For example, if you have a drinking problem or a kidney problem, what approach do you take to solving the problem? A visit to the doctor or a conversation with a loved one will mostly be the response. But have you ever thought that, somewhere in your mind, you've certainly seen some signs, symptoms or patterns that have made you register the fact that you have a problem? Only after the fact has been registered in your mind, subconsciously or consciously, do you seek for assistance which might be medical, advisory or emotional support from loved ones.

Claiming and accepting that you have a problem might not sit well with you if you can't find any issues wrong with you health-wise. That's where you need to look inward and check for subtle signs and symptoms that you might have been ignoring for so long. Good things about taking a proactive approach to cleansing your body are the massive benefits your body will gain from such a decision and activity. Either way, the result is the same a benefit your body and mind will always thank you for.

Taking a proactive measure to detoxifying helps with eliminating not only the toxins in our bodies but also nurturing them back to the default state if done correctly. Engaging in a cleansing and detoxing program helps the body in many ways. It changes our perception and approach to our eating behaviors causing us to become conscious of what we expose our bodies to and what we ingest inside our body. It changes our lifestyle for good.

Detoxification is about cleansing and nourishing the body from the inside out. By removing and eliminating toxins, you leave room for healthy nutrients to work efficiently. Detoxifying helps protect your body from disease and renews your ability to maintain optimum health.

Toxins & Toxicants

Toxins

Toxins are biological substances created by the body that is harmful to our health. They are mostly produced during the metabolism and growth of microorganisms in our bodies and if left unchecked can have a disastrous effect. The medicines we use can quickly turn from healer to killer when used in doses that are higher than what is recommended and what the body can accept. The latter definition can also be applied to the consumption of nutrients.

Toxins are not new. The body is exposed daily to toxins in the environment, during our vital bodily functions, and so on.

Thanks to our robust detoxifying organs, most of these toxins are destroyed or their effects neutralized and flushed out of the body before they can cause any significant harm to our bodies.

Toxicants

Toxicants, on the other hand, are similar to toxins in that they both cause damage to the body. A toxicant is any toxic substance produced by human activities. Toxicants could also refer to pollutants with poisonous potentials that are toxic to the human body depending on the duration of exposure (acute or long), route of delivery (inhalation, oral or dermal (skin)) and magnitude (doses or concentrations). These include pesticides, heavy metals, pollutants, etc.

Signs and Symptoms of Toxicity

As with every illness or disease, there are telltale signs and symptoms which help in successful diagnosing and treatment of the disease. Most signs and symptoms that accompany toxicity are listed below.

Skin issues

▶ Hormone imbalances

▶ Weight gain

▶ Fatigue

▶ Diabetes

▶ Obesity

▶ Bad breath

▶ Constipation

▶ Stress and negative emotions

▶ High blood pressure

▶ Osteoporosis

▶ Sleeping disorders

▶ Persisting exhaustion

▶ Loss of mental clarity and motivation

▶ Worsening inflammatory problems

▶ Susceptibility to flu and colds

▶ Back and joint pain

Diseases Linked to Toxicity

Below are some of the diseases found by researchers to be associated with toxicity, which is a great reason to keep our bodies healthy and safe from toxins.

- Parkinson's Disease
- Alzheimer's Disease
- Autism
- Depression and other mood disorders
- Insomnia
- Heart disease
- Cancer
- Fibromyalgia
- Arthritis
- Food allergies
- Menstrual problem –PMS, menopausal symptoms, mood changes and hot flashes
- Stroke

Toxins Pathway into the Body

Toxins enter our bodies through any of the exposure routes listed below.

1. **Inhalation**–Lungs
2. **Ingestion**–Digestive system
3. **Physical contact/Absorption**–Skin

Body Burden

Body Burden refers to the total accumulation of toxins in one's body. It's the sum total of little toxic compounds or substances in our bodies which can put too much strain on our health. With every product produced, there's a possibility of it being contaminated, and our exposure to these products and the polluted environment generally means we have a lot of toxins coming our way. Hence, our need to take a proactive measure in ensuring we don't get put down by diseases linked directly or indirectly to these toxins by strengthening and giving our detoxifying organs the boost it needs to function at its optimal level. Reducing our body burden should always be our priority.

Eliminating Toxins

When it comes to eliminating toxins in the body's systems, there are two approaches. I believe both are not mutually exclusive.

The first approach entails avoiding contact with toxins. This means that we are to be conscious of our activities and ensure we avoid the exposure of our bodies to toxins. The first approach is mostly concerned with deliberate efforts on our part. The second approach to dealing with toxins involves supplying our organs with needed nutrients required to efficiently get rid of toxins while reducing the strain on them through healthy eating habits.

The First Approach

The first approach involves making sure the toxins don't get to us in the first place. This approach is feasible in that it requires an understanding of toxins (and toxicants), their source, method of delivery, and in what concentration, dose or quantity are they lethal to our body. While you might not have access to some of the information about its concentration or don't have the time to research, a good place to start is knowing the primary source.

Sources of toxins/toxicants in the household include synthetic pesticides, synthetic fragrances, cleaning products, non-stick cookware/bakeware, flame retardants, vinyl, canned food, volatile organic compounds (e.g., laundry detergents), dry cleaning chemicals (containing perchloroethylene or PCE), beauty and personal care products.

Common Office Toxins

Sources of toxins/toxicants in the office include heating devices (when inappropriately used or when malfunctioning), machines and engines, and products with formaldehyde such as;

▶ Floor covering (varnishes, linoleum, plastics), fire retardants

▶ Paper products–envelopes, grocery bags, paper towels, disposable sanitary products

▶ Beauty products–cosmetics, deodorants, shampoos, fabric dyes, disinfectants, etc.

▶ Pressed wood products–particle board, plywood paneling, fiberboard, particleboard, etc.

While these lists are in no way exhaustive, they do give us a hint on various sources of toxins commonly found in our homes and workplaces.

The fact remains that we cannot eliminate the possibility of coming into contact with toxins, unless we take things to the very extreme, which this book is not intended. What we can do is try to be conscious and mindful of how we expose ourselves to the environment and objects with which we come into contact.

The food we eat, the manner in which we eat them, the quality (in terms of nutrition) and quantity also affect the buildup of toxins in the body. There is wisdom in the adage that states, "You are what you eat". Avoid eating refined sugars which are full of empty calories and are known to cause a spike in insulin which increases your chances of developing Type II diabetes, heart disease, obesity, acne, etc. Avoid eating excess fats such as the trans- and monosaturated kinds of fats as they increase your LDL cholesterol and increase your blood pressure.

The Second Approach

The second approach covers the effort channeled to helping our detoxifying organs carry out their function effectively and efficiently. Detoxification is carried out by some organs in our body such as the liver, kidneys, skin, lungs, etc. These organs along with the digestive and lymphatic systems all play vital roles in getting rid of toxins from the body.

These organs, especially the liver and kidneys, can only work on so many toxins at a time without becoming overwhelmed. When we eat unhealthily, we place more strain on the organs and give them no room for rejuvenation. This can be costly as their performance and effectiveness might reduce. Such reduced performances can give room to the gradual accumulation of toxins with nothing to stop them. The result can be devastating and could lead to a problem with the kidneys, liver, skin and other detoxifying organs or systems.

In this book, we will go through everything you need to know on cleansing your body and making informed decisions when it comes to detoxifying. You will be taught the tested and proven detoxifying program that has helped many people and read about results and glowing testimonials on achieving their detoxifying goals. These goals come with many benefits such as glowing skin conditions, improved vitality and energy level, weight loss and so on.

What to Expect During A Detox Process

During a cleansing program, the body undergoes a lot of changes. You may experience some changes and sensations in the body that were not present before as a result of the effect of the detoxing process. These are very common. Such side effects include changes in bowel movement, energy loss, fever, vomiting, dizziness, and loss of taste, etc. In most cases, the presence of these symptoms indicates a positive cleansing process. Each person is different and what one experiences might be different from another.

Below are some of the side effects (classified into degree) associated with a detoxification program.

Table 1: Side effects associated with a detox program

LOW	MODERATE	STRONG
Cold and flu-like symptoms	Symptoms of bronchitis or pneumonia	Paralysis of any part of the body
Fever	Discharges of mucus from the nose	Black mucus discharges from the lungs
Cough	Joint pain	Loose teeth

LOW	MODERATE	STRONG
Clear and yellow mucus discharge from nose	Changes in urine color to brown, orange or dark yellow	Diarrhea
Minor aches and pains	Pain in old injuries or degenerative areas of the body	Hearing loss
Slight vertigo	Minor paralysis of limbs	Vision loss
Watery stool	Chronic fatigue symptoms	Severe dizziness (or vertigo)
Energy loss	Nosebleeds	Severe fatigue
Rashes and itching	Severe dizziness (or vertigo)	Abscesses developing all through the mouth
Disease symptoms increasing temporarily	Severe fatigue	Loss of fingernails or toenails
Energy Loss	Mental confusion	Excessive weight loss
Mild headaches	Abscesses developing all through the mouth	Severe shortness of breath
Minor blurred vision	weight loss	Mental confusion
Minor vertigo	Depression or anxiety	Skin cracking
Weight loss		
Chills		

I've noticed throughout my career that it's rare for someone to reach the point of experiencing the moderate to strong side effects. The exception is organ damage to some extent. The body is also a factor here because each body is different and will react differently during the detoxing program.

What to Expect After a Detoxification & Cleansing Process

Each member that decided to join me in my detoxing program all had different outlooks, expectations and results. This is a compilation of the results

◗ Increased energy level, productivity level and vibrancy

◗ Weight loss

◗ Increased blood circulation

◗ Glowing/Clear skin

◗ Heightened sense of awareness–improved smell, taste, and hearing

◗ Tumor reduction or elimination

◗ Clarity in thinking

◗ Normalisation of blood sugars and blood pressure

◗ Improved state of mind

◗ Improved metabolism rate

◗ Improved bodily function

Organs Responsible For Detoxification

Introduction time. Meet the guys that form what I call the "Detox League". They are smart, hardworking, and loyal. Their cooperation is the reason while you are healthy, fit and can get away with indulging in some pleasurable yet unhealthy habits. They are always there to protect you.

Now don't indulge in unhealthy eating habits thinking the Detox League is invincible or insurmountable. You would only end up weakening their defense and performance. You don't want that. While every individual has a unique Detox League with various powers, they are not indomitable and the more you task them, the more they have to work and work with little time for a proper rest. Your body requires your Detox League to function at all times though not at the same activity level.

Even though this set of great guys dedicate their time to guarding you against harmful substances, they still have a life outside of guarding you. Once in a while, a little fight here and there can be good for them apart from their training to keep them fit and abreast of current situations happening in the body. When you keep getting into harm's way, relying on the Detox League to help save the day, you are overtaxing them as well as putting them in danger. As stated before, a lot of functions are placed in harm's way to indulge your taste buds and satisfy your cravings.

Because of the overtaxing, the Detox League once rumored to be indomitable is nothing more but a shadow of itself now. It wouldn't have made a difference to you if not for the fact that your system is paying for it dearly with fatigue, headache, and other health issues.

THE DETOX LEAGUE

▶ Liver

▶ Kidneys

▶ Lungs

▶ Lymphatic systems

▶ Skin

The Liver

The liver is a large, meaty organ located in the upper right portion of the abdomen, beneath the diaphragm and above the stomach. It is one of the most important organs in our body when it comes to ridding it of toxins. One of the primary functions of the liver peculiar to detoxification is to filter the blood coming from the digestive tract before it is passed to the rest of the body for circulation. The liver helps to metabolize drugs and detoxifies harmful chemicals.

The liver detoxifies the body of harmful substances by a complex series of chemical reactions. The liver contains various enzymes that help to convert fat-soluble (substances do not dissolve in water except in fat or oils) toxins into water-soluble substances that can be excreted in the urine or the bile depending on the particular characteristics of the end product.

The toxic chemicals that enter the body are mostly fat-soluble. This makes it difficult for the body to excrete them. Fat-soluble chemicals have a high affinity (attraction) for fatty tissues and cell membranes. The fatty tissues in the body act as a good hiding spot for these toxins. The toxins might accumulate in these fatty tissues for years in our bodies until they are broken down during exercise or when there's a need for energy with no carbs available.

The liver changes harmful metabolic byproduct in the body into unharmful substances that are excreted into the urine by the kidneys. The function of the liver is vast as it also helps in breaking down drugs and alcohol. It is responsible for breaking down insulin and other hormones in the body, protein synthesis, manufacturing of cholesterol and triglycerides, production of carbohydrate, stimulation of food digestion, conversion of glucose to glycogen and so much more.

The liver's detoxification process includes two steps:

Fig 1: The Liver Detoxification Phases

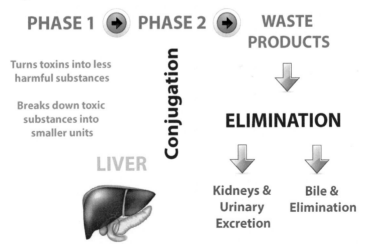

PHASE 1 ➡ **PHASE 2** ➡ **WASTE PRODUCTS**

Turns toxins into less harmful substances

Breaks down toxic substances into smaller units

Conjugation

LIVER

ELIMINATION

Kidneys & Urinary Excretion

Bile & Elimination

Detoxification Phases

In the liver cells, there are two major detoxification pathways which are called the Phase I and Phase II detoxification pathways.

In Phase I, toxins are either neutralized or converted into smaller units that make it easier for the next neutralization processes and handed over to Phase II.

Phase I

During this phase, the liver neutralizes toxic chemicals by converting them into smaller units that make it easy for enzymes in Phase II to act upon and excrete. In Phase I, some toxic chemicals are neutralized while the rest are turned into less toxic chemicals. During this conversion, free radicals are produced. In large quantities, free radicals can cause excessive damage to the liver. To avoid this, the liver uses antioxidants available to neutralize them before they can cause damage. During this detoxification process, the abundance of antioxidants to neutralize the free radicals produced during the conversion of harmful toxic substances into harmless or less harmful ones is very important. A lack of antioxidants could spell trouble for you as free radicals are known to cause cancers, tumors and a lot of other diseases. If not taken care of, it can accumulate and start wreaking havoc.

Nutrients needed by our body to carry out the Phase I detoxification process include:

▶ Antioxidants, e.g.,Vitamin (A, C, E), carotenoids (such as beta-carotene, lutein, and lycopene)
▶ B-Vitamins, e.g., B6 and B12

- Folic acid
- Glutathione

Toxins acted upon in this phase include:

- Metabolic End Products
- Contaminants/Pollutants
- Drugs
- Micro-Organisms
- Food Additives
- Insecticides
- Pesticides
- Alcohol

Phase II

In this phase, the substances (toxic) acted upon in Phase I are turned into a water-soluble substance through a series of processes and reactions. It involves forming conjugates that comprise toxic substance and chemical groups that help to neutralize toxins from Phase I.

For Phase II detoxification, the liver cells require sulfur-rich amino acids. The nutrients glycine, glutamine, choline, and inositol are also needed for efficient Phase II detoxification.

Nutrients needed by the body to carry out the Phase II detoxification process include:

- Sulphur, rich amino acids (e.g. glutamine, glycine, cysteine, and taurine)
- Phytochemicals (e.g. ellagic acid, isothiocyanates, glucosinolates, organosulfur compounds, curcumin, flavonoids, monoterpenes, etc)

The Kidneys

The kidneys are a pair of bean-shaped organs on either side of our spine, located below the ribs and behind the belly. The kidneys help to filter the fluid in the body, excreting urine in the process. This ensures that waste does not build up in the body.

The renal artery is responsible for carrying the blood to the kidney where it gets filtered. The urine formed after the filtration passes down the ureter to the bladder.

The kidneys are in charge of regulating the body's salt and acid content. They also help in regulating blood pressure. The kidneys also produce hormones that affect the function of other organs. Hormones produced by the kidneys help to regulate blood pressure and control calcium metabolism.

Fig 2: The Kidney (Bio.classes.ucsc.edu, 2012)

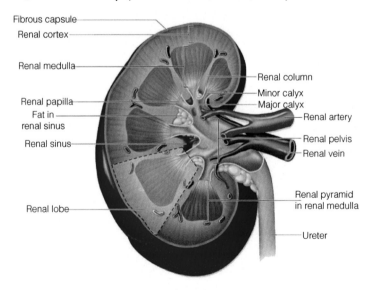

Fibrous capsule
Renal cortex
Renal medulla
Renal papilla
Fat in renal sinus
Renal sinus
Renal lobe
Renal column
Minor calyx
Major calyx
Renal artery
Renal pelvis
Renal vein
Renal pyramid in renal medulla
Ureter

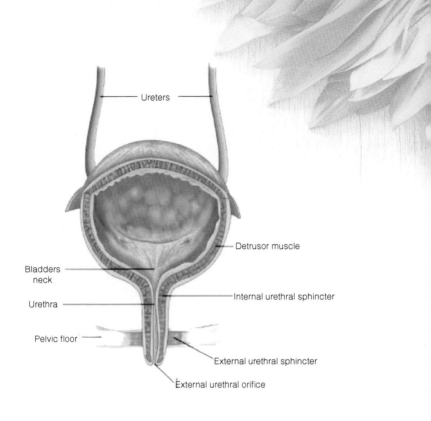

Ureters

Detrusor muscle

Bladders neck

Urethra

Internal urethral sphincter

Pelvic floor

External urethral sphincter

External urethral orifice

Functions of the Kidneys

▶ Maintain water and salt balance in the body

▶ Maintain proper osmolality

▶ Maintain proper plasma volume

▶ Help maintain a pH balance: proper acid–base balance in the body

▶ Excreting (eliminating) the end products (wastes) of bodily metabolism, e.g., ammonia

▶ Excreting foreign substances from bodywaste

▶ Erythropoietin production

▶ Renin production

▶ Converting vitamin D into its active form

Fig 3: Urine Formation (Mader, 1997)

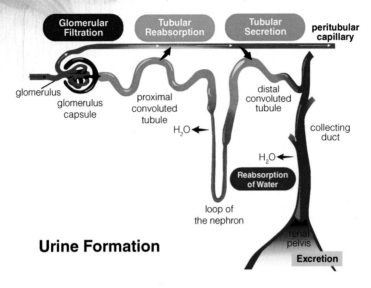

Urine Formation

The four processes involved in urine formation:

1. Glomerular Filtration
2. Reabsorption
3. Secretion
4. Excretion

The Lungs

Located in the chest, the lungs comprise a pair of spongy, large air-filled organs that are used for gaseous exchange between the blood in the body and the air outside the body. The lungs help excrete carbon dioxide—a waste product from the body.

Each lung is made up of sections called lobes. The lungs' primary purpose is to bring oxygen into the body and to remove carbon dioxide.

Diagram of the Human Lungs

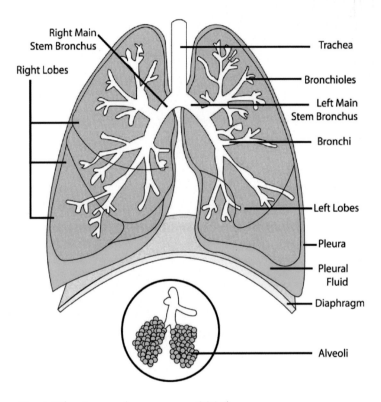

Fig 4: The Lungs (cancer.org, 2016)

During the process of breathing, air goes into our lungs through the nose (which is the preferred way of taking in air) or through the mouth. The air passes through the trachea which divides into the bronchi which have tiny air sacs at its ends called alveoli. The alveoli absorb oxygen from the inhaled air and remove carbon dioxide from our body which is expelled through our lungs when exhaling.

The diaphragm is responsible for forcing the movement of air in and out of the lungs by contracting (during inhalation) and relaxing (during exhalation).

The Lymphatic System

The Lymphatic System

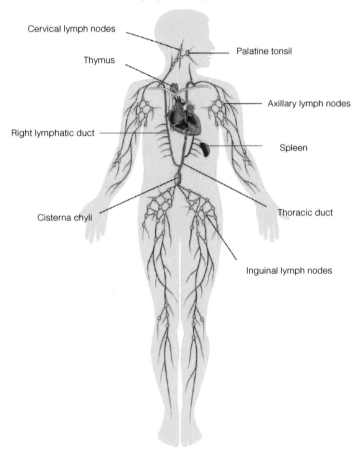

Fig 5: The Liver Detoxification Phases
(Lymphcareusa.com, 2017)

The lymphatic system is made up of a network of lymph nodes, lymph vessels and lymphatic capillaries spread throughout the body.

The lymphatic vessels act as a passage between our lymphatic system and our immune system. They are responsible for returning, filtering and concentrating excess fluid in our tissues back into the body's circulatory system. The lymph nodes act as "watchmen" on the lookout for toxins. The lymph nodes contain immune cells that help in detecting and destroying bacteria, cancerous cells and toxins. The lymphatic system plays a vital role in immune function by transporting lymph, a fluid containing infection-fighting white blood cells throughout the body.

Skin

The skin is one of the body's initial defense against external bacteria, viruses, and other microbes. The skin also protects the body from harmful ultraviolet radiation.

It is the largest organ of the body. It covers the body and comprises of three primary layers: Epidermis (outer) layer, dermis layer, and hypodermis layer. Our skin contains sweat glands that help our bodies in excreting waste via the skin surface through the regulation of sweat made up of urea, salts, and water.

The skin also acts as a layer that protects our body from external and foreign objects. The synthesis of Vitamin D is also a function of the skin among other functions.

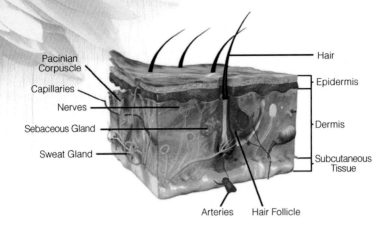

Fig 6: The Liver Detoxification Phases

Nutrition & Metabolism

The process of ingesting food and absorbing the nutrients available in the food is known as *Nutrition*. According to the online Merriam-Webster dictionary, Nutrition is *the act or process of nourishing or being nourished.*

Anything that nourishes the body is known as a "nutrient". We need nutrients for survival and growth.

Nutrients

Nutrients can be classified into six groups:

▶ Carbohydrates

▶ Protein

▶ Fats and oils

▶ Vitamins

▶ Minerals

▶ Water

They can be further classified based on their size and energy; (1) Macronutrients and (2) Micronutrients.

Macronutrients are nutrient required and consumed in large quantities such as Carbohydrates, Protein, and Fats whereas micronutrients, as the name suggests, are nutrients required and consumed in smaller quantities by the body. Examples include Vitamins and Minerals. Both macronutrients and micronutrients are essential to the body as they work hand-in-hand to ensure the body functions properly. A deficiency in any of the nutrients can lead to a health problem.

CARBOHYDRATES

Carbohydrates are the sugars, starches, and fibers found in grains, cereals, milk products, vegetables and fruits we eat. They are one of the macronutrients and the primary provider of energy to the body. At the chemical level, they contain carbon, hydrogen, and oxygen, hence, the name carbohydrates. They are an essential structural component of living cells and source of energy for animals.

Forms of Carbohydrates

Based on their chemical structure, absorption and digestion rate, we have two types of carbohydrates:

◗ Simple carbohydrates

◗ Complex carbohydrates

◗ Simple Carbohydrates (monosaccharides)

These include monosaccharides (single sugars) and disaccharides (two sugars). These carbohydrates are quickly absorbed and digested by the body. Due to their quick absorption rate and energy release rate, they can lead to spikes in blood sugar levels and cause a spike in insulin when consumed in large quanitities.

Table 2: Examples of Monosaccharide

Examples	Sources
Glucose	Vegetables, honey, fruits, cereal, cake, and sugar, etc.
Fructose	Fruits, fruit juices, high-fructose corn syrup, honey and maple syrup
Galactose	Milk, yogurt and ice cream

Examples	Sources
Ribose (RNA)	Fruits and vegetables
Deoxyribose (DNA)	Fruits and vegetables

Table 3: Examples of Disaccharide

Examples	Sources
Maltose	Bread, potatoes and malt grains etc.
Lactose	Milk and dairy products, chocolate, nougat, instant potatoes, salad dressing, etc.
Sucrose	Refined beets, ketchup, flavored yogurts, candy, cookies, ice cream and sugar cane, etc.

Complex Carbohydrates (polysaccharides)

Complex carbohydrates (polysaccharides) have three or more sugars. They are often referred to as starchy foods and include potatoes, corn, whole-grain, parsnips, bread and cereals etc.

Polysaccharides, when hydrolyzed, yield over twenty monosaccharides. Polysaccharides include two groups: starch, and cellulose.

Table 4: Examples of Polysaccharide

Example	Sources
Starch	Wheat, Maize (Corn), Rice, and Cassava, etc.
Cellulose	Cabbage, Brussel Sprouts, Broccoli, Collard Greens, Kale, Cauliflower, etc.

Table 5: The Recommended Daily Amount (RDA)

Typical values	Women	Men	Children (5-10 years)
Calories	2,000 kcal	2,500 kcal	1,800 kcal
Protein	45 g	55 g	24 g
Carbohydrate	230 g	300g	220 g
Sugars	90 g	120 g	85 g
Fat	70 g	95 g	70 g
Saturates	20 g	30 g	20 g
Fiber	24 g	24 g	15 g
Salt	6 g	6 g	4 g

According to the National Institute of Health (NIH), 45% to 65% of total daily calories consumed should come from carbohydrates.

A gram of carbohydrate equals four calories. So if your daily calorie intake is approx.1800, then 45%–65% which is within the range of 945 calories (236g) to 1365 (341g) calories. Depending on your medical history, your carb intake might differ, and it's advisable to consult with your doctor should you plan on going on a diet or changing your diet plans.

Function of Carbohydrates

1. Primary source of energy
2. Provides and stores energy needed by the body to carry out its bodily functions
3. Essential for brain function
4. Maintenance of the integrity of nervous tissue
5. Availability of carbohydrates prevent ketosis

Good Carbs, Bad Carbs?

According to some school of thought, there is no such thing as good or bad carbohydrate. They may be correct to some extent, but when it comes to carbs, they are wrong. There are good carbs and bad carbs. And no, it doesn't come with a label or sign. Both are sumptuous and tastes good.

So how do you differentiate between both? A good way to differentiate between both of them is using a simple checklist. Identifying good or bad carbs is much more difficult than this but I hope you get the gist from the little table I used.

Table 6: Good Carbs vs Bad Carbs

Good Carbs	Bad Carbs
Low or moderate in calories	High in calories
Devoid of refined sugars and refined grains	Contains refined sugars and grains
High in fiber	Has little to no fiber
Low in sodium	High in sodium
Devoid of cholesterol and trans fat	High in cholesterol and trans fat

Carbohydrate Metabolism

It is paramount as humans to maintain glucose concentration within a narrow, normal range. Carbohydrate metabolism begins with digestion in the small intestine where glucose is absorbed into the bloodstream. Blood sugar concentrations are controlled by three hormones: insulin, glucagon, and epinephrine. These hormones have different roles to play. Insulin facilitates and stimulates the uptake and storage of glucose by the liver and the muscle when blood sugar is high.

The metabolic process *glycogenesis* is responsible for converting excess glucose into glycogen which is stored in the liver and muscles until it's needed by the body. When our blood glucose level is low or we are in situations that demand we have more glucose at our disposal (such as when running away from something that can cause you harm, fighting etc), the epinephrine and glucagon hormones do the reverse of what the insulin does; they release glucose back into the body through a metabolic process known as *glycogenolysis*. The metabolic process responsible for providing immediate supply of energy from the consumption of food is called *glycolysis*.

- Glycolysis – Formation of pyruvic acid or lactic acid. Releases energy for the body in the form of ATP
- Glycogenesis – formation of glycogen from glucose
- Glycogenolysis – conversion of glucose to glycogen

Deficiency in Carbohydrates

What happens when our carb intake is low?

- Hypoglycemia (known as low blood sugar)
- Ketosis
- Acidosis
- Fatigue and decreased energy levels
- Unhealthy weight loss
- Dehydration and reduced body secretions

- Loss of sodium
- Weakened immune system
- Constipation
- Mood swing

Carbohydrates Overdose

What happens when our carb intake is higher than we need?

- Weight gain
- Insulin resistance
- High blood sugar level
- Low HDL Cholesterol Level

PROTEINS

Proteins are a derivative of amino acids. The body synthesizes amino acids to create what we call protein. Proteins are essential nutrients. They are large, complex molecules comprising of one, two or more long chains of amino acids held together by peptide bonds, i.e., polymer chains made up of amino acids linked together by peptide bonds. As the building blocks of body tissue, proteins play a critical role. They help the body regenerate new cells, repair tissues, organs and so much more. They also serve as a secondary source of energy in the unavailability of carbohydrates and fat.

There are nine (9) essential amino acids not synthesized by the body and need to be obtained from our diets for the proper functioning of the body.

These amino acids include:

- Phenylalanine
- Tryptophan

- Valine
- Threonine
- Isoleucine
- Methionine
- Leucine
- Lysine
- Histidine.

A deficiency in any of these amino acids could lead to malnutrition, health problems which could result to death if the deficiency persists.

Amino acids that can be synthesized by the body without the need to obtain them from our diet includes:

- Alanine
- Glutamic Acid
- Aspartic Acid
- Asparagine And
- Serine.

The best sources of amino acids are found in plants. Plant proteins include anything from legumes, nuts, and grains etc.

Functions

- Antibodies which are specialized proteins helps to protect the body from antigen (toxins, enzymes or foreign substances) by neutralizing them e.g. Phenylalanine
- Enzymes helps in catalyzing chemical reaction

- Messenger proteins serve as chemical messengers between cells e.g. hormones
- Structural provides structure and maintenance for cell shape.
- Provide the nutrients needed for cell and tissue growth
- Used by the body in cellular and tissue generation and regeneration
- Utilized in the formation of hormones, nucleic acid, co-enzymes, etc.
- Utilized in the formation of blood cells
- Certain proteins help in transporting ions and small molecules across a membrane
- Storage helps to store amino acids for later use

Deficiency in Amino Acids

What happens when our amino acid intake is low?

- Slow Metabolism
- Low Immunity – more susceptible to diseases
- Muscle Atrophy – decrease in muscle mass
- Difficulty with weight loss
- Slow tissue injury repair
- Muscle, bone, and joint pain
- Low energy levels
- Fatigue
- Poor concentration and trouble learning
- Erratic Moods
- Unstable blood sugar levels
- Kwashiorkor (in severe cases)
- Marasmus (in severe cases)

Amino Acid Overdose

What happens when our amino acid intake is high?

) Smelly breath
) Kidney problems
) Glycemic index issues
) High cholesterol
) Weight gain

Amino Acid Metabolism

Series of processes involved in amino acid metabolism include:

) Deamination and transamination of amino acids, followed by conversion of the non-nitrogenous part of those molecules to glucose or lipids
) Removal of ammonia from the body by synthesis of urea. Ammonia is a toxic substance that can wreak havoc if not flushed out of the body quickly and efficiently. It could lead to a central nervous system disease among other diseases.
) Synthesis of nonessential amino acids needed by the body

Digestive and Metabolic Products of Amino acids

End Products

) Protein
) Glucose (Gluconeogenesis)

Toxic By-Products

◗ Uric acid

◗ Urea

◗ Ammonia

◗ Nitrogen compounds (nitrates, etc.)

◗ Ketones

FATS

Fat, alongside carbohydrates and proteins, makes up the three major macronutrients needed by the body to function. They provide energy and aid in the absorption of fat-soluble vitamins such as fats, oils, and triglycerides.

Unlike carbohydrates and proteins that provide four calories per 1 gram, fat provides nine (9) calories per gram. They are the next source of energy when carbohydrates are unavailable.

Oil, Fat, and Lipid

◗ Oil refers to fat with short or unsaturated fatty acid chains that are liquid at room temperature.

◗ Fat refers to fats that are solids at room temperature.

◗ Lipid is a general term that includes fats, oils, and triglycerides.

Types of Fats

◗ Trans-Fat

◗ Saturated Fat

◗ Unsaturated Fat

Trans-Fat

Fats that have undergone hydrogenation are called trans-fat. Trans-fats usually have a higher shelf life and are harder at room temperature due to the hydrogenating process they undergo. When consumed in high quantity, trans-fat can raise the level of our cholesterol. It's advisable to stay clear from trans-fat whenever possible. In cases where it could not be avoided, eat as little as possible if it cannot be avoided.

Trans-fat is usually found in cookies, margarine, salad dressings, processed foods, foods with hydrogenated oils or shortening.

Saturated Fat

Any fat solid at room temperature is known as "saturated fats". They are known as solid fats. Saturated fat is mostly found in animal foods such as milk, cheese, and meat. They are also found in tropical oils such as palm oil, cocoa butter, and coconut oil. Saturated fat can raise your cholesterol. A healthy diet has less than 10% of daily calories from saturated fat.

Unsaturated Fat

Unsaturated fats are fats that are liquid at room temperature. They are mostly in oils from plants. According to research, eating unsaturated instead of saturated fat might help improve your cholesterol levels.

Fatty Acids

Fatty acids are the building blocks of fats, just as amino acids are the building blocks of proteins. Fatty acids, when combined with glycerol, produce fats.

Essential Fatty Acids

Linoleic acid and alpha-linolenic acid are two essential fatty acids needed by the body. As the body is unable to synthesize them, they need to be obtained from the food we eat. Sources of alpha-linolenic acids include vegetable and nuts.

Linoleic acid—Promotes healthy skin and hair growth, healthy brain function and required for bone density, etc.

Linolenic acid—Promotes nerve and brain function, regulates inflammation, etc.

Functions of Fats

▶ They are used as storage units for energy (triglycerides).

▶ They provide protection for our internal organs in the form of padding.

▶ Fats assist with the utilization of fat-soluble vitamins (including A, D and E).

▶ They are involved in maintaining proper body temperature.

▶ Used in the development and function of the brain.

▶ They help guard against internal heat loss

▶ Omega 3 fats are anti-inflammatory

▶ Fats helps promote healing.

▶ Strengthen nerve tissues and nerve response.

▶ Involved in the manufacture of hemoglobin which helps to transform oxygen from the lungs to our body tissues.

▶ Omega 3 Fats helps to nourish and protect the skin.

Sources of fats

◗ Margarines

◗ Nuts

◗ Cheese (Plant Based).

◗ Avocados

◗ Seeds

Fat Metabolism

The following describes the process of fat digestion and metabolism:

1. Emulsification
   Bile Salts emulsify fats and make them water–soluble so that pancreatic and intestinal lipase can convert them to fatty acids and glycerol.

2. Conversion
   Gastric juices and the enzyme steapsin converts fats into fatty acids and glycerol (alcohol).

3. Binding
   Fatty acids bind with transport protein and lipoproteins

4. Transportation
   The bound fatty acids are taken to where they are needed.

Digestive and Metabolic Products of Fats

End Products

◗ Essential fatty acids

◗ Fatty acids

◗ Glycerol (alcohol)

◗ Glycerides

◗ Water

Toxic By-Products

- Carbon dioxide
- Ketones (toxic to diabetic patients in high levels)

Deficiency in Fat

What happens when our fatty acids intake is low?

- Dermatitis – skin inflammation
- Psychological and neurological disorders e.g. depression
- Low absorption of fat-soluble vitamins
- Cardiovascular diseases
- Auto-Immunity and chronic inflammation:

Fat Overdose

What happens when our fatty acid intake is high?

- Atherosclerosis – narrowing of the arteries
- Increased cancer risk
- Risk of obesity
- Brain injury
- Increased risk of heart disease
- Increased cholesterol level

VITAMINS

Specific groups of organic compounds essential in small quantities for healthy growth, metabolism, development, and bodily function are known as *vitamins*. Like amino acids, some vitamins can be synthesized by the body while others need to be obtained from our diets. There are 13 vitamins needed by the body to function properly. Each vitamin has specific jobs.

Types of Vitamins

▶ Water–soluble

▶ Fat–soluble Vitamins

Water-Soluble Vitamins

Water-soluble vitamins are vitamins that dissolve in water. They are easily absorbed into the bloodstream. Examples include Vitamin C (ascorbic acid), and the B vitamins (thiamin, riboflavin, niacin, vitamin B6, vitamin B12, folate, pantothenic acid, and biotin).

While it is easy to be deficient in water-soluble vitamins, it is rare for water-soluble vitamins to be at toxic levels which is dangerous to the body as the body only takes up what it needs and the kidneys filter excess from our bloodstream which is excreted in urea. Water-soluble vitamins are not stored in large amounts in our bodies; once our bodies has taken what it needs, the rest is excreted.

Table 7: Functions of Vitamins and their Sources (Dietitians of Canada, 2013).

Vitamin	Function	Food Sources
Vitamin B1 (Thiamin)	Helps with energy production in your body	Whole grains, enriched grains, liver, pork, dried beans, nuts and seeds

Vitamin	Function	Food Sources
Vitamin B2 (Riboflavin)	Helps with energy production in your body. Helps your body use other B vitamins	Soybeans, meat and poultry, liver and eggs, mushrooms, milk, cheese, yogurt whole grains, enriched grains
Vitamin B3 (Niacin)	Helps your body to use protein, fat and carbohydrate to make energy. Helps enzymes work properly in your body	Mushrooms peanut butter, meat, fish, poultry whole grains, enriched grains
Biotin	Allows your body to use protein, fat and carbohydrate from food	Sweet potatoes, nonfat milk, yogurt peanuts, almonds, eggs, liver, soy protein *The biotin content in food can vary greatly*
Vitamin B6 (Pyridoxin)	Helps your body to make and use protein and glycogen which is the stored energy in your muscles and liver. Helps form hemoglobin which carries oxygen in your blood	Potatoes, bananas, 100% bran, instant oatmeal, meat, fish, poultry, liver, soybeans, chickpeas, lentils, pistachio, nuts, sunflower seeds

Vitamin	Function	Food Sources
Vitamin B12 (Cobalamin)	Works with the vitamin folate to make DNA Helps to make healthy blood cells. Low levels of vitamin B12 can cause a type of anemia. Keeps nerves working properly	Milk, cheese, yogurt, fortified soy or rice, beverages, meat, fish, poultry, liver, eggs, fortified soy products
Folate	Helps to produce and maintain DNA and cells Helps to make red blood cells and prevent anemia Getting enough folic acid lowers the risk of having a baby with birth defects like spina bifida.	Asparagus, cooked spinach, romaine lettuce, Brussels sprouts, beets, broccoli, corn, green peas, oranges, orange juice, bread, enriched pasta, wheat germ, liver, dried beans, soybeans, chickpeas, lentils, sunflower seeds, flaxseeds * Folic acid is the type of folate found in Vitamin supplements and fortified foods.

Vitamin	Function	Food Sources
Vitamin C	May help prevent cell damage and reduce risk for certain cancers, heart disease and other diseases Helps heal cuts and wounds and keeps gums healthy, Protects you from infections by keeping your immune system healthy Increases the amount of iron your body absorbs from some foods	Citrus fruits such as oranges, grapefruits and their juices, kiwi, strawberries, mangoes, papaya, red, yellow and green peppers, broccoli, Brussels sprouts, tomatoes, raw dark leafy vegetables
Vitamin A	Helps you to see in the day and at night Protects you from infections by keeping skin and other body parts healthy Promotes normal growth and development	Liver, some fish, milk, cheese

Vitamin	Function	Food Sources
Carotenoids:	Carotenoids are not vitamins but some types can turn into vitamin A in the body. Act as antioxidants which protect your body from damage caused by harmful molecules called free radicals	Cantaloupe, pink grapefruit, tomatoes, broccoli, dark green leafy vegetables like spinach, beet greens and Swiss chard, dark orange vegetables such as carrots and sweet potatoes
Vitamin D	Increases the amount of calcium and phosphorus your body absorbs from foods Deposits calcium and phosphorus in bones and teeth, making them stronger and healthier Protects against infections by keeping your immune system healthy	Milk, fortified soy and rice beverages Fortified margarine Some fish, eggs, organ meats, fish liver oils
Vitamin E	Helps to maintain a healthy immune system and other body processes Acts as an antioxidant and protects cells from damage	Vegetable oils, Avocados, leafy green vegetables, wheat germ, sunflower seeds, some nuts, peanut butter
Vitamin K	Makes proteins that cause our blood to clot, when you are bleeding Involved in making body proteins for your blood, bones and kidneys	Broccoli, soybeans, dark green leafy vegetables such as kale, collards, turnip/ beet greens and spinach

Table 8: Vitamins Deficiency and Symptoms

Vit.	Disease	Symptoms
	Deficiency	
A	Night Blindness	Inability to see clearly in dark places
B1	Beriberi	Shortness of breath during physical activity waking up short of breath rapid heart rate swollen lower legs.
	Brain Disorder (Wernicke-Korsakoff syndrome)	double vision, a drooping upper eyelid, up-and-down or side-to-side eye movements, loss of muscle coordination a confused mental state
B2	Ariboflavinosis	Red, itchy eyes, Night blindness Cataracts, Migraines, Peripheral neuropathy, Anemia , Fatigue Malignancy
	Glossitis	Pain in the tongue, tongue swelling, change in the tongue color to pale or fiery red, difficulty in speaking, eating, or swallowing
	Angular Cheilitis	Bleeding, swollen, cracking Blistering, crusting, itching or/and scaly painful corner of the mouth
B3	Pellagra – Hartnup Disease	Skin rash, anxiety, rapid mood swings, delusions, hallucinations intention tremor, speech difficulties, sensitivity to light etc.
B5	Paresthesia	Numbness, weakness, tingling, burning, cold

Deficiency		
Vit.	Disease	Symptoms
B6	Depression	Fatigue, Feelings of guilt, aches, overwhelming sadness, , pains, worthlessness, and helplessness, overeating/appetite loss, cramps, Pessimism and hopelessness, Insomnia, Irritability, Restlessness etc.
	Dermatitis	
B7	Cheilitis, Glossitis, depression, insomnia	Symptoms include brittle hair /hair loss, dry scaly skin, , , hallucination, dry eyes, loss of appetite, fatigue etc.
B9		Fatigue, gray hair, mouth sores tongue swelling, growth problems
B12		Tingling in the feet and hands extreme fatigue, weakness irritability or depression etc.
C	Scurvy	Anemia, painful joints and muscle, in the muscle or bone depression, mood swing, teeth loss, gum diseases, loss of appetite, mood changes, and depression etc.
D	Rickets	Skeletal deformities – bowlegs, curved spine etc, teeth deformities, pain or tenderness in the bones of the arms, legs, pelvis, or spine, stunted growth and short stature, bone fractures and muscle cramps etc.
E		Muscle weakness, muscle atrophy, vision problems
K		Bruises easily, small blood clots underneath the nails, black stool (might contain blood), bleeding in the mucous membrane.

	Overdose and Side Effects	
Vit.	**Diseases**	**Symptoms**
A	Hypervitaminosis A	Blurry vision or other vision changes, bone pain, poor appetite, dizziness
B1		nausea and vomiting, sensitivity to sunlight, dry, rough skin, itchy or peeling skin, cracked fingernails, skin cracks at the corners of your mouth, mouth ulcers, yellowed skin (jaundice), hair loss, respiratory infection, confusion
B2		Side – effects: diarrhea, orange-tinted urine, sun-induced eye damage, itching or numbing sensations
B3	Niacin Overdose	Severe skin flushing combined with dizziness, Rapid heartbeat, Itching Nausea and vomiting, Abdominal pain Diarrhea, Gout
B5		Diarrhea
B6		
B7		
B9		
B12		
C		Side – effects: headache, cramps, nausea, diarrhea, dental decalcification, vomiting, heartburn, abdominal bloating, insomnia and Kidney stones, rectal bleeding

Overdose and Side Effects		
Vit.	Diseases	Symptoms
D	Hypercalcemia	Headaches, fatigue, excessive thirst, excessive urination, nausea, abdominal pain, decreased appetite, constipation, vomiting, bone pain, osteoporosis, fractures from disease
E		Side Effects: headache, nausea, stomach cramps diarrhea, , fatigue , blurred vision, skin rash bruising and bleeding etc.
K		Jaundice in newborns, hemolytic anemia, and hyperbilirubinemia.

Note: conditions, disorder are all termed diseases by the author as there exist a thin line between their definitions and meaning. For easy comprehension and to avoid confusion, diseases was used.

*** Side effects are usually amplified by high doses.

MINERALS

Minerals are substances (nutrients) found in our food that our bodies need for proper growth, health and the proper functioning. There are two forms of minerals: (1) Macro minerals and (2) Trace minerals.

Macrominerals as the name implies means the minerals needed by our bodies in large quantity. They include phosphorus, calcium, potassium, magnesium, sodium, and chloride. Trace minerals are minerals needed in small quantity by our bodies. Examples include iron, fluoride, copper, iodine, zinc, and selenium.

Table 9: Minerals, Benefits and Souces

Mineral	Benefits	Sources
Calcium	Needed for forming bones and teeth Helps nerves and muscles function	Canned salmon with bones, sardines, milk, cheese, yogurt, Chinese cabbage, kale, collard greens, turnip greens, mustard greens, broccoli, and calcium-fortified orange juice.
Chloride	Needed for keeping the right amount of water in the different parts of your body	Salt, seaweed, rye, tomatoes, lettuce, celery, olives, sardines, beef, pork, and cheese.
Copper	Helps protect cells from damage Needed for forming bone and red blood cells	Organ meats, shellfish (especially oysters), chocolate, mushrooms, nuts, beans, and whole-grain cereals.
Fluoride	Needed for forming bones and teeth	Saltwater fish, tea, coffee, and fluoridated water.
Iodine	Needed for thyroid gland function	Seafood, iodized salt, and drinking water (in regions with iodine-rich soil, which are usually regions near an ocean).
Iron	Helps red blood cells deliver oxygen to body tissues Helps muscles function	Red meats, poultry, fish, liver, soybean flour, eggs, beans, lentils, peas, molasses, spinach, turnip greens, clams, dried fruit (apricots, prunes, and raisins), whole grains, and fortified breakfast cereals.

Mineral	Benefits	Sources
Magnesium	Needed for forming bones and teeth Needed for normal nerve and muscle function	Green leafy vegetables, nuts, bran cereal, seafood, milk, cheese, and yogurt.
Phosphorus	Needed for forming bones and teeth Needed for storing energy from food	Milk, yogurt, cheese, red meat, poultry, fish, eggs, nuts, peas, and some cereals and bread.
Potassium	Needed for normal nerve and muscle function Needed for keeping the right amount of water in the different parts of your body	Milk, bananas, tomatoes, oranges, melons, potatoes, sweet potatoes, prunes, raisins, spinach, turnip greens, collard greens, kale, most peas and beans, and salt substitutes (potassium chloride).
Selenium	Helps protect cells from damage Needed for thyroid gland function	Vegetables, fish, shellfish, red meat, grains, eggs, chicken, liver, garlic, brewer's yeast, wheat germ, and enriched bread.
Sodium	Needed for normal nerve and muscle function Needed for keeping the right amount of water in the different parts of your body	Salt, milk, cheese, beets, celery, beef, pork, sardines, and green olives. (Many people get too much sodium. For tips on cutting back, see Reducing your sodium.)

Mineral	Benefits	Sources
Zinc	Needed for healthy skin Needed for wound healing Helps your body fight off illnesses and infections	Liver, eggs, seafood, red meats, oysters, certain seafood, milk products, eggs, beans, peas, lentils, peanuts, nuts, whole grains, fortified cereals, wheat germ, and pumpkin seeds.

Table 10: Minerals Deficiency and Overdose

Mineral	Deficiency	Overdose
Zinc	Zinc Deficiency	Zinc Toxicity
Selenium	Selenium Deficiency	Selenosis
Molybdenum	Molybdenum Deficiency	Molybdenum Toxicity
Manganese	Manganese Deficiency	Manganism
Iron	Iron Deficiency	Iron Overload Disorder
Iodine	Iodine Deficiency	Iodismhyperthyroidism
Phosphorus	Hypophosphatemia	Hyperphosphatemia
Sodium	Hyponatremia	Hypernatremia
Magnesium	Hypomagnesemia,	Hypermagnesemia
Potassium	Hypokalemia	Hyperkalemia
Chlorine	Hypochloremia	Hyperchloremia
Calcium	Hypocalcaemia	Hypercalcaemia
Copper	Copper Deficiency	Copper Toxicity
Cobalt		Cobalt Poisoning
Chromium	Chromium Deficiency	Chromium Toxicity

WATER

Water is an important part of the body. In fact, it makes up more than 60 percent of our body weight.

Functions of water:

▶ Moistens tissues, such as those around your mouth, eyes, and nose
▶ Keeps our body hydrated
▶ Aids in Digestion
▶ Regulates helps in regulating our body temperature
▶ Serves as a cushions for our joints
▶ Helps the body get nutrients
▶ Flushes out waste products from the body

Deficiency in Water

What happens when our water intake is low?

▶ Dehydration
▶ Fluid and Electrolyte Imbalances
▶ Problems with Temperature Regulation
▶ Dizziness

Water Overdose

What happens when water intake is high?

▶ Water intoxication
▶ Muscle weakness, spasms, or cramps
▶ Unconsciousness

Hormones and Metabolism Regulation

To maintain homeostasis, there is a need for metabolism regulation. We have two types of metabolic hormones; anabolic hormones and catabolic hormones.

The primary anabolic hormone being insulin increases in the blood after a meal rich in carbs and proteins. Insulin activates the storage enzymes in our bodies, signaling the cells to take up glucose, fatty acids, and amino acids. When the body has more than what it needs for immediate use, it converts it into glycogen, triglycerides, and body protein. Insulin encourages intake and storage of nutrients.

Catabolic hormones are responsible for the breaking down of stored nutrients such as triglycerides, glycogen, and body proteins for energy. These hormones include glucagon, epinephrine, and cortisol.

Whenever our blood glucose drops, there is a rise in the concentration of glucagon as it signals the body to release the glucose from the glycogen stored in the body.

Epinephrine, also known as adrenaline, is a hormone secreted by the medulla of the adrenal glands. It is released during exercise or in response to a fight or flight situation. Epinephrine stimulates the breakdown of stored energy reserves, i.e., glycogen.

Cortisol is a hormone that is released during stress. Cortisol provides the body with glucose by tapping into protein stores via gluconeogenesis in the liver.

Table 11: Hormones and Metabolism

Metabolic State	Hormone	Site of Secretion	Role in Carbohydrate	Role in Lipid Metabolism	Role in Protein Metabolism	Overall Metabolic Effect
Fed	Insulin	Pancreatic beta cells	Increases cell uptake of glucose Increases glycogen synthesis	Increases synthesis and storage of triglycerides	Increases cell uptake of amino and protein synthesis	Anabolic
Fasting	Glucagon	Pancreatic beta cells	Increases glycogen degradation Increases gluconeogenesis	Increases lipolysis	Increases degradation of proteins	Catabolic
Exercise	Epinephrine	Adrenal medulla	Increases glycogen degradation	Increases lipolysis	No significant effect	Catabolic
Stress	Cortisol	Adrenal cortex	Decreases cell uptake of glucose Increases gluconeogenesis	Increases lipolysis	Decreases cell uptake of amino acids increases degradation of proteins	Catabolic

Free Radicals & Antioxidants

Free Radicals

Free radicals are atoms or molecules that have unpaired electrons that are usually unstable and highly reactive. The use of the element O2 known as oxygen for the generation of energy leads to the production of free radicals. Free radicals are not as evil as some people in the health industry paint them to be.

Free radical is a norm and necessary to carry out bodily function. In low concentration, they play a role in cellular response and immune function as they act as defense; neutralizing toxic and foreign substances (invaders) in the body by oxidizing them. They also play a role in physiological processes. Free radicals are important. When the concentration of free radicals is high, causing an imbalance between them and the antioxidants in the body, they generate oxidative stress, a harmful process which can damage cell structures.

Formation of Free Radicals

Reactive Oxidative Species (ROS) and Reactive Nitrogenous Species (RNS) are two types of free radical in the body. ROS and RNS are internally or externally formed/derived in the body. Internally derived free radicals are generated from immune function, cell metabolism, inflammation, infection, mental stress, degenerative diseases such as cancer. Externally derived free radicals result from the metabolism of environmental pollution, heavy metals, alcohol, drugs, cigarette smoke, alcohol, industrial solvents, cooking (smoked meat, used oil, fat), radiation etc.

Toxic Activities of Free Radicals in the Body

Oxidative stress can alter the cell membrane and other structures such as proteins, lipids, lipoproteins, and deoxyribonucleic acid. Free radicals such as ROS attacks the liver as the parenchymal cells in the liver are subjected to oxidative stress which causes injury.

Oxidative stress has been linked to and known to play a role in the development of chronic and degenerative ailments. Examples of such ailments include cancer, arthritis, cardiovascular and neurodegenerative diseases, aging and autoimmune disorders, etc.

One of the most significant sites of free-radical damage is the cell membrane. Free radicals that form within the phospholipid bilayer of cell membranes steal electrons from their stable lipid molecules. When the lipid molecules, which are hydrophobic, are destroyed, they no longer repel water. With the cell membrane's integrity lost, the ability to regulate the movement of fluids and nutrients into and out of the cell is also lost. This loss of cell integrity causes damage to the cell and all systems affected by this cell.

Other sites of free-radical damage include low-density lipoproteins (LDLs), cell proteins, and DNA. Damage to these locations disrupts the transport of substances into and out of cells, alters protein function, and can disrupt cell function because of defective DNA. These changes may increase our risk for chronic diseases such as heart disease, various cancers, diabetes, cataracts, Alzheimer's disease, and Parkinson's disease.

What Are Antioxidants and How Does the Body Use Them?

For the past three decades, antioxidants have been the stars for the health industry. Virtually every supplement in the market or drug has a form of antioxidant or the other. The addition of an antioxidant to health products holds such an appeal that no company can resist not including it in their label.

So what are antioxidants? Are they the real thing? The hope, as we are made to believe, or just a hype? What are their roles in our bodies? What do they do when it comes to detoxification?

Antioxidants

Antioxidants are natural substances whose job is to clean up free radicals in the body by donating electrons to highly reactive and unstable free radical, which helps to reducing its damaging capacity. Antioxidants are just like conflict mediators that helps resolve issues before it escalate into violence or war. They behave in similar fashion as they interact with free radicals and help terminate chain reaction process before vital molecules are damaged.

Antioxidants need to be restored constantly in the body to avoid oxidative stress as an antioxidant becomes oxidized when it destroys a free radical.

Antioxidants such as glutathione, uric acid, bilirubin and melatonin are endogenous antioxidants i.e. they are produced during metabolism in the body. Exogenous antioxidants unlike endogenous antioxidants cannot be synthesized in the body and are to be obtained from our diets. Such antioxidants are also known as nutritive anti-oxidants and they include carotenoids, vitamin E & C, trace minerals (selenium, manganese, zinc), omega-3 and omega-6 fatty acids etc.

How Do Antioxidants Work?

Antioxidants are believed to work in two ways:

1. Stabilizing the free radical through donation of an electron to the free radical

Fig 8: Anti-Oxidant and Electron Donation

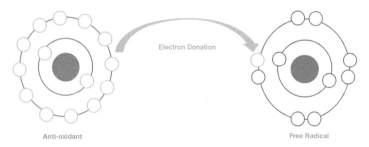

Electron Donation

Anti-oxidant   Free Radical

2. Removing the free radical initiator by "scavenging" initiating free radicals or by stabilizing transition metal radicals such as copper and iron

Levels of Antioxidant Action

Antioxidants are one of the first lines of defense the body employs to keep free radicals in check and prevent them from damaging other cells. The antioxidants function at different levels as we have those that try to prevent the formation of radicals (preventive), those that scavenge for free radicals (scavengers) in the body, those that repair the cell from the damage caused by free radicals (repairer) and those that tend to signal the synthesis and transportation of antioxidants to the site of formation for free radicals.

In general, antioxidants try to remove free radicals or stabilize them by doing everything they can which includes donating an electron for stabilization, scavenging for free radicals, inhibiting its formation or binding with it to neutralize its effect and render it harmless after which it can be flushed out of the system.

Endogenous and exogenous antioxidants act as "free radical scavengers" by preventing and repairing damages caused by ROS and RNS, and therefore can enhance the immune defense and lower the risk of cancer and degenerative diseases.

NUTRITIONAL ANTIOXIDANTS

There are three main types of nutritional antioxidants:

1. Vitamins & Minerals
2. Phyto-chemicals and
3. Enzymes

VITAMINS & MINERALS

Examples: Vitamins A, C, E, folic acid, and beta-carotene.

Source: orange, grape, carrot, banana, lemon, liver, milk

Vitamin A is essential for improving the immune system, eye health, tissue repair, and cholesterol levels.

Vitamin E is essential for maintaining healthy blood vessels, improving skin conditions, and protecting our body's membrane. Vitamin E is stored in the lipid portion of our cell membranes. It act as an antioxidant by donating an electron to free radicals, protects the lipid molecules in our cell membranes from being oxidized and stops the chain reaction of oxidative damage.

Vitamin E, once oxidized, is excreted from the body. In some cases, however, the oxidized antioxidant is recycled back through the help of other antioxidant nutrients, e.g., Vitamin C into active vitamin E.

Vitamin C is a water-soluble antioxidant that helps to protect our skin from UV damage, provides greater resistance to infections and contributes to regulation of our blood cholesterol. Vitamin C prevents the damage of cells and tissues by donating electrons to free radicals. It also protects LDL cholesterol from oxidation, which may reduce the risk for cardiovascular disease. It enhances immune function by protecting the white blood cells from the oxidative damage that occurs in response to fighting illness and infection. Vitamin C also helps in regenerating vitamin E after it has been oxidized by free radicals .

Fig 9: Anti-Oxidant Recycling

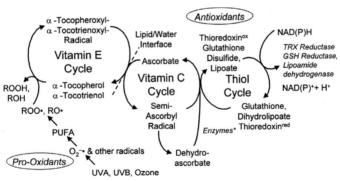

Dehydroascorbic acid is also regenerated as an antioxidant by gaining an electron from the reduced form of glutathione (GSH). Glutathione is also restored to its antioxidant form by the enzyme glutathione reductase in a reaction that is dependent on the mineral selenium.

Beta-carotene is an organic red-orange pigment found in plants and fruits. It is commonly found in orange-colored vegetables like carrots, pumpkins, sweet potatoes, and dark green vegetables like spinach, kale, and collards. It is a powerful carotenoid that protects our bodies against free radicals.

Coenzyme Q10 is a substance produced by the body for basic functioning of cells. A decrease in the production of coenzyme has been linked to the development of various age-related diseases and conditions. The decrease in coenzyme has an direct relationship with our age i.e. as we get older, our production of coenzyme Q10 deceases.

Selenium

Selenium is a mineral that contributes to antioxidant activities. It forms the active site of several antioxidant enzymes including glutathione peroxidase that protect our bodies from oxidative damage. The biochemical function of glutathione peroxidase is to reduce lipid hydroperoxides to their corresponding alcohols and to reduce free hydrogen peroxide to water.

Selenium in trace quantities is vital to our health. Selenium and vitamin E work together to prevent oxidative damage to lipids and decrease damage to our cell membranes. Selenium plays a role in immune function. It is involved in the maintenance of body temperature and basal temperature.

There are numerous antioxidant enzyme systems in our bodies. Copper, zinc, and manganese are a part of the superoxide dismutase enzyme complex. Iron is part of the structure of catalase. These minerals also play major roles in the optimal functioning of many other enzymes in the body.

PHYTOCHEMICALS

Phytochemicals are chemical substances produced by plants with antioxidant properties. Example include: Carotenoids, Flavonoids, Allyl sulphides, Polyphenols etc.

ENZYMES

Superoxide dismutase, catalase, and glutathione peroxidase are examples of the antioxidant enzyme systems. They are made from the protein and minerals in the food we eat. Superoxide dismutase helps in the conversion of free radicals to less damaging substances such as hydrogen peroxide.

The catalase further works on the hydrogen peroxide and converts it to water and oxygen. Glutathione peroxidase helps in scavenging and inactivating of hydrogen and lipid peroxides. It also removes hydrogen peroxide from the body and stops the production of free radicals in lipids.

For antioxidant enzymes to provide optimum antioxidant activity, they require cofactors such as iron, copper, selenium, magnesium, and zinc. The quality of the protein source does have an impact on the quality of the antioxidant enzymes.

Sources of Antioxidants

Most natural whole foods, such as whole grains, fruits, and vegetables, contain phytochemicals; whereas processed or refined foods contain little to no phytochemicals.

Table 12: Antioxidants and their Sources

Antioxidant	Source
Allium Sulphur Compounds	Leeks, Onions, Garlic
Anthocyanins	Eggplant, Grapes, Berries
Beta	Carotene, Pumpkin, Mangoes, Apricots, Carrots, Spinach, Parsley
Catechins	Red Wine, Tea
Copper	Seafood, Lean Meat, Milk, Nuts
Cryptoxanthins	Red Capsicum, Pumpkin, Mangoes
Flavonoids	Tea, Green Tea, Citrus Fruits, Red Wine, Onion, Apples
Indoles	Cruciferous Vegetables such as Broccoli, Cabbage, Cauliflower
Isoflavonoids	Soybeans, Tofu, Lentils, Peas, Milk
Lignans	Sesame Seeds, Bran, Whole Grains, Vegetables
Lutein	Leafy Greens Like Spinach, Corn
Lycopene	Tomatoes, Pink Grapefruit Watermelon
Manganese	Seafood, Lean Meat, Milk, Nuts
Polyphenols	Thyme, Oregano
Selenium	Seafood, Offal, Lean Meat, Whole Grains
Vitamin C	Oranges, Blackcurrants, Kiwi Fruit, Mangoes, Broccoli, Spinach, Strawberries

Antioxidant	Source
Vitamin E	Vegetable Oils, Avocados, Nuts, Seeds, Whole Grains
Zinc	Seafood, Lean Meat, Milk, Nuts
Zoochemicals	Red Meat, Offal, Fish

The 30-Day Detox Program

A detox program, well-structured and realistic in day-to-day application, can go a long way in helping fight against and rid your body of toxins. A good detox program provides the body with the nutrients that fight back and work to their optimal level while limiting the body's exposure to toxins.

The fundamental building blocks of any detoxification program should include - NEHMB:

(Healthy) Nutrition

▌ To flush out toxins and reintroduce nutrients into the body

Exercise

▌ Keeps the body fit and in an active state

Heat Induced Sweating - A sauna, steam room

▌ Helps in relaxing your muscle (sauna) and detoxifying your body (steam)

Meditation

▌ Help relax the mind reduces stress levels

Body work

▌ Pain relief, increased vitality etc.

The 30-day cleansing program is broken into a series of days which make up a phase. Each phase has its benefits and challenges. The program was designed to integrate easily into your daily routine and lifestyle. The first few days can be tough as your body needs to adjust and adapt. It's normal, so brace yourself for impact. It should be noted that the time to adapt varies across people as it depends on your body and will.

By the time you finish the 30-day detoxing program, your achievement and success will be something that puts a smile on your face.

*Note: While this book contains a lot of rich information on health and detoxing, enrolling in the 30-day detox program is advisable as you get superb support, close monitoring, in-depth information tips and a community that keeps you motivated.

JUICE FASTING

Juice fasting is a type of fast that involves consuming only fruit and vegetable juices and water with no solid foods for a period of time.

The juice enriches the body with polyphenols that are rich in various antioxidants and other potential health benefits. Antioxidants protect the body from oxidative stress damage. Juice fasting also helps in eliminating unhealthy eating and drinking habits such as overeating, eating junk food, drinking large amounts of alcohol, etc.

During a juice fasting, the liver and kidneys undergo lesser strain as they process less toxic substances from ingested foods and can focus more on ridding the body of toxins.

Juice fasting helps to burn fat which can help release any toxins stored in fat cells. The liver, when functioning properly, can effectively remove the released toxins from the body.

Juice fasting can be traced to the Ayurveda medicine practice.

PHASE

1

Days

1 – 3

Cayenne pepper

Sea Salt

Syrup

Key Lime

The first three days of your detoxing program consist of a cycle that involves doing a salt water flush every morning and taking a limeade drink throughout the day. The salt water flush helps to get rid of toxins by stimulating the liver and also for better absorption of nutrients. The limeade drink is to provide nourishment and a sort of refreshment for your body throughout the day.

The sea salt water is done every morning after waking up and before taking anything as the flush is more effective on an empty stomach with nothing to block its absorption. During this period, you are not to take any solids as that would forfeit the aim of taking in liquid alone. Whenever you feel hungry, drink your limeade water.

In a situation where you were tempted or in a situation that made you take in solid, you would have to start this phase all over again. So don't get tempted or put yourself in a situation in which you'd need food.

In most cases, after a salt water flush, you will start experiencing the need to use the toilet which can be in minutes after taking the salt water or half an hour. It all depends on your body.

Celtic Salt Water Flush

A salt water flush, also known as a master cleanse, helps you to cleanse your colon and digestive system by bringing about a forced bowel movement,

Salt is needed for many biochemical processes, including (but not limited): adrenal gland/thyroid gland function, cell wall stability, muscle contractions, nutrient absorption, nerve stimulation, pH, and water balance regulation.

Salt water flush helps to force your digestive system to release stored waste in the body, however little (or a lot) there might be.

Salt helps to balance hormones, facilitates with metabolic processes and establishes an optimal pH level in the body.

Benefits

- Eases sore throat
- Cleans wound
- Lowers pain in inflamed muscles
- Provides trace minerals
- Clears fluid retention
- Balances hormone
- Establishes optimal pH Level
- Forces out toxins and cleanses the colon
- Balances electrolyte/mineral levels
- Facilitates metabolic processes
- Clears up digestive issues

Nuggets:

A salt water cleanse should always be performed in the morning on an empty stomach prior to engaging in any activity for the day advisable it's taken the moment you wake up as it gives you enough time for toilet use without affecting your daily routine.

How to Perform a Salt Water Flush

Steps:

Step 1: Pour 2 teaspoons of celtic sea salt into a full cup of lukewarm water.

Step 2: Stir vigorously to ensure the salt dissolve very well

Step 3: Drink the full cup

Step 4: Repeat Step 1 – 3 for a total of three times

*Note: Should you be unable to drink anymore (stomach full), continue with drinking warm water.

Don't:

Never take a solid during this phase not before the salt water flush and certainly not after.

Maple and Cayenne Limeade Drink:

Makes 1 Serving

- 10 ounces of distilled water
- 1/10 of teaspoon of cayenne pepper,
- 2 Tablespoons of grade A or B maple syrup
- 2 Tablespoons of fresh key lime juice

*Note: Drink 6 to 12 glasses a day for the entire period.

Key Lime is high in vitamin C and negative ions– a great antioxidant that helps protect the body against free radicals and its harmful effects. The cayenne pepper helps rev up the body's metabolism. Maple syrup is rich in a lot of minerals – calcium, iron, magnesium; vitamins – thiamin, riboflavin, niacin, and B6. It is a good source of zinc and manganese which plays a vital role in the strengthening of our immune system.

Nuggets:

Laxative or Peppermint Tea: Peppermint tea is meant to help cure nausea and soothe the stomach. An herbal laxative tea can also be drunk before bed to stimulate digestion and clean the system of toxins.

Going the Extra Mile:

Added Activities to Help Detox:

1. Sauna – Steam sauna is best. Sit for 10-20 mins or whatever your body will allow you to handle. Follow with a cold shower/rinse to close pores.

Benefits

▶ Relieves stress
▶ Relaxes muscles and soothe aches/pains in both muscles and joints
▶ Cleanses the skin
▶ Recreational and social benefits
▶ Helps burn calories
▶ Helps fight illness
▶ Makes you feel good about yourself which helps reduce depression

2. Exercise – Get moving by doing low impact activities like walking, jogging, biking, light weight lifting, etc.

Benefits

▶ Improves mood
▶ Reduces stress
▶ Boosts Energy
▶ Helps combat health conditions and diseases
▶ Helps control weight
▶ Increases relaxation

▶ Increases stamina

▶ Decreases risk of injury

3. Lymphatic Drainage Massage — Help drain your lymph naturally of waste fluids

Benefits

▶ Reduces swelling and detoxification of the body

▶ Regeneration of tissues and cells

▶ Improves the function of the immune system

▶ Stretching — Reduces risk, increase performance

PHASE II

DAYS

4 – 7

Dandelion Tea

Coconut

Thai Coconut

The Detox

You've successfully completed the first phase. You deserve a treat! Go watch a movie and have fun. Don't load up on solids or do anything detrimental to what we are trying to accomplish.

So this is basically the beginning of Phase II. Welcome Back!

By now you would have noticed some changes. Your breath, your stool and yeah, your weight. The cravings would have also hit the roof by now. It's okay to have this cravings and desire for food, just don't give into temptation. You are stronger than that!

I'm not saying this to make you happy. No. For some people, the first three days are hell and that's where they give up. For you to reach Phase II means you really want this and I believe in that strength. Guess what? You will complete this phase.

From day four to day seven, our ideal liquid is coconut water due to its freshness and refreshing taste. Drink only when hungry. Your tea shouldn't be left out just because you have a new flavor. Tea contains antioxidants and helps with the stimulation of digestion and flushes out toxins.

Nuggets:

Young Thai coconut water has a sweeter taste and quenches your thirst.

Brown round furry coconuts are fine. Just be sure they have water and are not moldy.

Dandelion tea helps in weight loss; it is a powerful antioxidant and diuretic that helps eliminate toxins.

Coconut Water Benefits

- Lowers blood pressure
- Helps reduce weight
- Increases athletic performance
- Boosts energy levels
- Lowers cholesterol
- Relaxes muscle tension

Exercise:

Complete these upon waking up or before noon! This is to target the lymphatic system and continue to move toxins out of the body.

25 Jumping jacks OR

2 Mins of Jump Ride OR

3 Mins of Jumping Jacks

Do's:

Avoid the temptation of not wanting to exercise when it's due time.

Avoid trying to add up your exercise all at once with aim to do it once and have the other days free of exercise. Sorry, it doesn't work that way.

Going the Extra Mile:

Perform same activities in Phase I for added addictive for detoxification.

PHASE III

DAYS

8 – 11

Chlorophyll Water

Turnips

Mustard Greens

Spinach

Collard Greens

Key Limes

Kale

Well, you are here. I knew it wasn't gonna be that easy, but I also knew you would make it. By now, you should have gotten over most of the initial problem associated with the fasting. The coconut water was a godsend as you have seen.

So this is the third phase and things are going to get more interesting!

We are preparing our first green drinks. I know you can't wait to have a taste of it. Well, green drinks are just ways of saying you are going to be consuming chlorophyll water, dark greens and limes in the third phase of our detoxification process. You will either love it or hate it, but you still need to drink them.

Green Drinks

▶ Chlorophyll water (from crushed greens)
▶ Distilled water
▶ Dark greens (Turnip greens, spinach, kale, mustard greens, collard greens, etc.) Any or all at once can be used.
▶ Key Limes– helps to release the iron in greens

How to Prepare the Green Drinks

Step 1: Wash the greens with water thoroughly.

Step 2: Crush them up to release chlorophyll.

Step 3: Add the crushed greens and limes into the water.

Step 4: Allow it to sit in water overnight.

Voila! Our award-winning proprietary green drinks are available. Don't worry. You will get to be more flexible on what goes into your drinks. For now, be patient and work your way to the next phase.

Nuggets:

Once you remove your Green Drink from the refrigerator the next day, do not put it back in. It is best to drink at room temperature.

Key limes – Add key limes to water to continue to detox the body.

Continue drinking teas.

Exercise:

Complete these upon waking up or before noon! This is to target the lymphatic system and continue to move toxins out of the body.

25 Jumping jacks OR

2 Mins of Jump Ride OR

3 Mins of Jumping Jacks

Going the Extra Mile:

Add a multiplier to the exercise task. 1.2 to 1.5 is good. If you can do more, the better. But do not exert yourself too much to avoid exhaustion.

Multiplier: Multiply whatever you are doing by your chosen number which could be 1.5. for example, if you were performing a jumping jacks of 30 initially. Your multiplier being 1.5 will be multiplied by the number of jacks you do (30) which makes it 45.

Added Activities to Help Detox:

▶ Same as in Phase I.

▶ Add Colonics or colon hydrotherapy

PHASE IV

DAYS

12 – 15

Distilled Water

Turnips

Mustard Greens

Parsley

Red Kale

Collard Greens

Cilantro

Key Limes

Kale

Great! You made it to Phase IV.

Phase IV is an extension of phase III and contains some amazing twists. I'm adding more greens to your collection. You get to be picky.

ORGANIC ONLY – Makes 1 Serving a Day

◗ Collard Greens
◗ Red kale
◗ Green kale
◗ Dandelion Greens
◗ Mustard Greens and/or Turnip Greens
◗ Italian Parsley
◗ Cilantro
◗ Key limes
◗ Gallon of distilled water

Instructions

Take equal amounts of each green relate to each other and add limes to taste

Add to blender (Vitamix) and blend until liquid. ★★★ If you do not have Vitamix, strain liquid.

Pour and store in glass container and enjoy!!

Exercise:

Complete these upon waking up or before noon! This is to target the lymphatic system and continue to move toxins out of the body.

25 Jumping Jacks OR

2 Mins of Jump Ride OR

3 Mins of Jumping Jacks

+ Stairmaster Workout

Instruction – Stairmaster Workout:

Use the StairMaster for at least 25 min.

Select a speed that you can handle for 25 min as well as keep proper form.

Do not hold on, lie over machine or hold yourself up.

With each step, engage your glutes!

Stairmaster Benefits:

- Aerobic Conditioning
- Helps to burn calories
- Builds Strength
- Non – Impact

Alternatives to the Stairmaster Workout

Walk stairs at home, a stadium, bleachers, work etc.

Slow speeds to adjust setting to your comfort level

Going the Extra Mile:

Add a multiplier to the exercise task. 1.2 to 1.5 is good. If you can do more, the better. But do not exert yourself too much to avoid exhaustion.

Multiplier: Multiply whatever you are doing by your chosen number which could be 1.5. For example, if you were performing a jumping jacks of 30 initially. Your multiplier being 1.5 will be multiplied by the number of jacks you do (30) which makes it 45.

Added Activities to Help Detox:

▸ Same as in Phase III.

▸ Add Colonics or colon hydrotherapy

PHASE V

DAYS

16 – 19

Tangerine

Papaya

Mango

Grapefruit

Kiwi

Pineapple

Apple

Strawberry

Apricot

So we are in Phase V and there's nothing new to tell you. Maybe, we should go back to drinking just limeade. What do you think?

Well, if you had consented to go back to drinking just limeade, then these fruit and vegetable combos are not for you. So here's the gist for those of us who waited and didn't consent, keep drinking teas and key limes just as in the previous phase to help with your body detoxification.

Tired of drinking the same green smoothie every time with different combos? Is it starting to taste boring and your taste buds are craving for something nice and delicious? Well, your wish was just granted.

We are going to be creating fruit drinks in this phase. The good thing is that we are grouping them. Therefore, you are free to taste different groups as long as they are not on the same day.

Instruction

Fruit Drinks! Each group has its own pairing. One group is considered one drink. Do not combine different groups within one day.

Enzyme Boost Blackberries, Black grapes (with seeds), Dates, Figs, Mango, Pineapple, Papaya, Coconut water, Aloe Vera (optional), Cantaloupe

Fibroid Killer   Black figs, Distilled water, Blackberries, 1 date

Blackroot Tonic

Start with the Enzyme boost or fibroid killer. For the enzyme boost you can add muscadine grapes with the black grapes.

Group 1	Kiwi, Pineapple, Papaya, Mango
Group 2	Grapefruit, Tangerine, Orange lime, Lemon
Group 3	Cranberry, Blueberry, Raspberry, BlackBerry, Mulberry, Elderberries, Strawberry
Group 4	Honeydew, Cantaloupe, Watermelon
Group 5	Grapes, Black currant, Pomegranate
Group 6	Peach, Plums, Apricots
Group 7	Apples, Pear, Prickly pear, Rose Apple
Group 8	Carambola, Guava, Passion fruit

Exercise:

Planks

- 2 min planks total of 6 minutes
- 2 front
- 2 left side
- 2 right side

Be sure to get sunlight two times a day hours of 6am–1130am 4pm–till sundown.

No hats, sunglasses, sun block, or anything blocking you from the sun like weaves/long sleeve clothing, etc. Get as much of your body exposed to the sun as possible!

StairMaster for 25 min

Select a speed that you can handle for 25 min as well as keep proper form.

Do not hold on, lie over machine or hold yourself up.

With each step engage your glutes.

Alternative

Walk stairs at home, a stadium, bleachers, work etc.

Slow speeds to adjust setting to your comfort level

Added Activities to Help Detox:

Sauna – Steam sauna is best. Sit for 10-20 mins or whatever your body will allow you to handle. Follow with a cold shower/rinse to close pores.

PHASE VI

DAYS

20 – 30

You have successfully reached the last phase in the 30-day detoxing program. How does it feel? From the very first day to this moment, what was the journey like? What did you have to give up? What did you achieve? How was the progress?

You know what? Hold onto your answers for a few more days. You've still got your best 11 days ahead of you to reach your health goal be it beauty, health, weight loss, improved energy levels and so on.

In this phase, we are introducing some yummy soups. You have the option of taking it along with your fruit ninja combo drink.

Navy Bean Soup

Ingredients

- 1lbs of navy beans
- 1 tsp. grape seed oil
- 1/2 scallion
- 1/2 green onion
- 1/4 red /green bell pepper
- 1 bouillon cube (Vegan)
- 1/2 tsp smoked paprika
- 1 tsp lime
- 1/2 cup diced tomatoes
- 1 cup water (or more)
- Pinch of sea salt
- 3 leaves of cilantro

Method of Preparation

- Soak beans for an hour
- Remove, rinse, then boil beans in a pot of water and sea salt until soft

- Chop scallions and red bell pepper. Sauce with 1 TB grape seed oil sea salt and pepper
- Sauté for 3-4 minutes.
- Add everything else to the blender.
- Add to pot and heat on med
- Stir well until hot.
- Then remove it from the stove
- Simmer for a few minutes then enjoy

Avocado Soup

Ingredients

- 1/2 scallion
- 1 tsp grapeseed oil
- Pinch of sea salt
- 1 vegan bouillon
- 1 avocado
- 1 cup coconut milk
- 3 Tbs coconut cream

Method of Preparation

- Saute scallion with oil and salt
- Add avocado in blender
- Add bouillon
- Add milk and coconut cream
- Blend all to your desired texture
- Then add to pot on med heat stir well until hot
- Remove from stove
- Let simmer

Then enjoy!

Butternut Squash Soup

Ingredients

- 1 Kabocha squash
- 1 butternut squash
- 1 tsp. Cinnamon
- 1 tsp Cardamom
- 2 tbs grapeseed oil
- 1 tsp. Vegan butter
- 2 tsp. Ginger
- 1 spoon of local honey
- 1/2 can of coconut crème
- 1/2 cup organic stock

Method of Preparation

- Cut butternut squash in half and scrape out the core section of seeds.

- Once complete, add both squashes to baking pan and Vegan butter and sea salt then cover pan with foil and bake at 350 degrees until soft.

- Combine all other ingredients and blend

- Check on squash and once soft remove from oven

- Scrape out the inside and add to blender (insides only, do NOT add skin)

- Now add squash to soup base blend again to desired texture and add to stove on medium until hot. Then remove from stove and let simmer. Enjoy!

- Garnish with coconut crème and green onions *optional (onions must be grinded real fine)

Exercise:

Planks

- 2 min planks total of 6 minutes
- 2 front
- 2 left side
- 2 right side

Be sure to get sunlight 2 times a day hours of 6am–1130am, 4pm-till sundown.

No hats, sunglasses, sun block, or anything blocking you from the sun like weaves/long sleeve clothing, etc. Get as much of your body exposed to the sun as possible.

StairMaster for 25 min

Select a speed that you can handle for 25 min as well as keep proper form

Do not hold on, lay over machine or hold yourself up

With each step engage your glutes

Alternative

Walk stairs at home, a stadium, bleachers, work etc.

Slow speeds to adjust setting to your comfort level

Added Activities to Help Detox:

Sauna – Steam sauna is best. Sit for 10-20 mins or whatever your body will allow you to handle. Follow with a cold shower/rinse to close pores.

THE END OF THE DETOX PROGRAM

Final Thoughts

Edmund Burke once said, "The only thing necessary for the triumph of evil is for good men to do nothing."

To apply the same quote here, I'd say to you right now that the only thing necessary for the triumph of toxins, poor health, and a myriad of health issues in your life is for you as an individual to do nothing about it. Wishful thinking or ignorance won't help you face the problem head on.

With the knowledge you have gained so far in regards to toxins their origin, nature and effect, nutrition and the role they play in the functioning of the body making an informed decision about healthy eating should be easy and become second nature to you.

The 30-day detox program is meant to help your detox system carry out its function optimally and hopefully reset your eating habits which can only be possible if you put in the effort.

I charge you with the task of taking a bold step and changing your approach to nutrition in a healthy way.

More Success Stories

"I really wanted to participate in the class. However, I was initially reluctant because I am currently breastfeeding my 2.5-year-old toddler and 6-month-old daughter. I know that detoxing and cleansing is normally advised against when breastfeeding. But, I still wanted to participate because I knew that it would be beneficial in the long run for mine and my baby's health.

I have a long history of using birth control, depression, anxiety, stress, fatigue, and lethargy, which all have negatively affected my overall health and wellness. For several years now, I have been taking small steps towards turning my health and lifestyle around, and I have been on my own personal campaign to becoming a more conscious consumer and also becoming my own physician, and choosing preventative medicine (starting in my kitchen) over western treatments and pharmaceuticals.

I was advised of the potential risks of choosing to go ahead with the cleanse, and was encouraged and guided towards slight modifications to help me with my personal situation. I initially was going to supplement my children's feedings with fresh nut milks, but my little girl wouldn't take the bottle. So, in the beginning I just monitored my children closely and was successful at flushing my system.

During the liquid flush with the herbs, I modified the herb list by omitting the herbs that stopped lactation and substituting them with herbs that were known galactogogs. The flush was revitalizing to say the least. There is something strangely satisfying about purging the body. My urine was eventually clear. I felt my body become more hydrated.

The green drinks take a little getting used to if you're not used to that kind of thing. But, as I began to regain energy I hadn't had since before my children, I became accustomed to the taste and even looked forward to it. Overall, the cleansing got me in tune with my body's natural cues for hunger and thirst, which, before the class were off for me. I hadn't realised before just how used to being dehydrated I was, which explained the lethargic overtones in my day to day.

Once we made it to the fruit juicing phase, I had noticed I wasn't as cranky or drowsy, and I didn't require a nap in the afternoon like I had before.

The group I was in was luckily very helpful and supportive. We all provided lots of support and feedback for one another. One of the things I learned that I value a lot is proper grouping of herbs, fruits, and veggies for the body. One of the hardest things when changing my lifestyle has been finding the right way to group things amidst all the information hearsay. There was a clear emphasis on the science behind what we were doing, rather than just weight loss.

I began the journey at 133 and very tired with fluctuating mood. I am happily at 128 and feeling very revitalized and refreshed. I also have more confidence when making healthy choices in the store and when it comes to making my own juices at home. I am very pleased. My children are fine and healthy, and breastfeeding is going strong. They seem to love their healthier, happier, more easy-going mama!"

Christina Rigaud

"I'll be honest. I really wasn't sure I could do this, so it has been more of a mental challenge for me than anything else. I'm 67 and although I've been plant-based for a few years, my weight is not at a good place. I've been up and down with that and I think a lot of it is because I haven't been combining foods correctly. I eat too many fruits and I love pasta, avocados, and almond butter! I wasn't on any meds when we started except for cortisone shots in my knees a couple times a year for severe arthritis. I also have lymphedema in both legs. Other than that my BP is good, but I have to be careful because it fluctuates to borderline high occasionally.

All of my friends are on numerous medications for various ailments that they attribute to old age. I am determined to keep on being the odd man out! I've lost 22 pounds but still have a long way to go to reach my goal. I have been teaching for many, many years and I can't recall a year when I did not come home every day completely exhausted, especially the first few weeks. This year was totally different. My mental clarity and mood have also been great and my arthritis isn't bothering me quite as much."

B. B

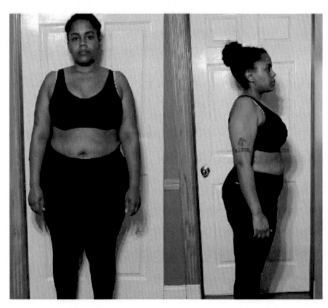

"I started the 30-day detox on Aug. 18, 2017. Besides being overweight, I have no major health issues and wasn't on any medication prior to doing the detox.

My main goal when starting this detox was to improve my metabolism, prepare my digestive system to absorb nutrients better and to get rid of parasites. While on the detox, I noticed a change in my complexion within the first 2-3 days. By day 3-4 my energy level had already greatly increased.

Early into the detox my menstrual cycle came on. Usually I would have a headache 1-2 days prior to its arrival but that didn't happen during the detox. I had very mild cramping the morning of; I expected the pain to increase but that never happened.

This was the first time in many years that I went without needing something for pain. Usually I have a 5 day cycle it was only 3 days during the detox.

About two weeks into the detox we were directed to get a colonic and that's exactly what I did. I was surprised to see that I wasn't packing tons of waste. I would like to think that day 1-3 of the detox helped tremendously with that.

I lost a total of 20.6 lbs during the detox and slowly gained 2 back near the end while consuming soups.

I really wish that I had taken a before picture on day one of the detox because I had already lost 13.4 lbs by the time I took my 1st photo. There's only about a 6-7 lb difference between these photos."

Anita Wright

I loved class. I love the detailed info provided and the delicious recipes. I love the information and knowledge provided from our instructor!

Days 1–3: Slight headache the first day; I vomited just a tad bit on that 3rd cup of salt water. Afterwards, all was well. I am non-active with exercising and I am currently 193 lbs.

Days 4–7: Coconut water really kept me afloat. Key Lime water, blaaah, it had my throat really dry. I was full of energy and there were no issues this period of time at all! Started losing weight around Day 5!

Days 8–11: These days were mentally the roughest for me. I did Cucumber/Spinach Chlorophyll water and Teas. I experienced hunger the most these days. Energy levels were lower than the other days. But still higher than prior to this fast! Start noticing the plaque feeling on the back of my teeth during this phase. I think it was from all the teas!

Days 12-15: Pounds started dropping for me a little more moving into this phase. I experienced an amazing boost of never ending energy. Whoever created The Green Giant juice blend is a genius and had a sister feeling like Hercules! I noticed a white patch on my tongue which was yeast starting this phase. On Day 14 my weight loss was 13 lbs total so I'm down to 180 lbs and I am full of energy

Days 16-19: Fruit drinks were so amazing and during this timeframe. I'm down to 175 lbs! The planks are a beast! Still doing teas, jumping jacks, and jump rope during this timeframe and full of energy.

Days 20-22: The Brazil and Walnut Milk taste good, even though I'm not a milk drinker. I was completely exhausted. My menstrual cycle was on and I was feeling weak. I had no pain and my menstrual was odorless! I even had my boyfriend to smell cause I was so shocked!

I did Organic Blackstrap Molasses as recommended by Chef Lightfoot El, for minerals which were lost from my menstrual and my energy was back up in no time! I also did the colonic hydrotherapy and mucus was found. No pathogens, no parasites found with that session, and no yeast. I felt lighter and mental clarity was at an all-time high! I felt really good about getting it done! I highly recommend this to anyone, male and female!

Days 23-30: All of the soup recipes were absolutely amazing! My total weight loss was 23 lbs which has me leaving this fast at a whopping 167 lbs! After having 5 babies. .youngest just turned 3. I have an 8, 9, 11, and 15 yr old. I had "flabby" skin on my lower abdomen and it has tightened! Doctors said this would most likely not happen!

They lied! Ha! My legs, thighs and arms are smaller and more toned! I can tell a huge difference in the way my body feels on the inside. I am so happy and I feel amazing and clean and I am so grateful for our great instructor even though he worked a nerve, but we probably worked his even more!

This is the 2nd class of his I have taken and I recommend any class he offers to anyone who is trying to obtain optimal health! I have taken a lot of notes and will use what I've learned for the rest of my life! This was an awesome experience with an awesome group of people!"

Takitta Ollison

"Yesterday was day 30 for me. This fast was amazing. It really showed me what I was made of. I never went longer than 10 days on a juice fast. It really is all mental. I woke up each day excited to see what changes were made in my body. My skin became so soft, I couldn't stop touching my skin. My face became so clear and blemishes began to fade.

Over time, I no longer had plaque build-up on my teeth. I would wake up with fresh breath and my teeth felt cleaned. I no longer had body odor, even after workouts, so I went without deodorant. My sleep was much deeper.

I lost 15 lbs (18 lbs at one point) by end of the fast and was able to maintain my weight loss when we added back in soup. Dropped 2 pants sizes. I felt my breathing slowed, almost like I was getting more quality air. Odd. Not really sure how to explain it. My cycle has been 2-3 days since becoming vegan but during the fast it became even lighter and was a total of 2 days with no spotting on the third day.

I did a colonic towards the beginning of the fast and passed parasites, mucus and candida. On the second colonic you could tell the detox was working. The water was mostly clear the whole time. I didn't have any issues with dandruff. I feel lighter and energetic. So happy I did this fast. I don't even crave sugar or carbs anymore. Actually the thought of it right now is a turn off."

Courtney Keen

"When I started the 30-day detox I wasn't sure I would complete it. I was overweight, my metabolism was slow and I was addicted to sugar and starches. My focus when starting this detox was to increase my energy and speed up my metabolism and hopefully expel some parasites as well. One thing I didn't consider was a change in my menstrual cycle.

While on the detox, I noticed a change in the length and flow of my cycle. Usually I have a 8-10 day cycle with 4-5 days heavy this time it was only 6 days with only 2 heavy days. My cramping was less painful but my attitude was more snappy.

I lost 15 lb total. I see it mostly in my face and stomach. I have more energy. During this fast, I learned better eating habits and how to successfully fast and nourish my body in the process.

Chef Lightfoot El was a great teacher and he held us accountable. We became a tribe, supporting and encouraging each other daily."

Chokmah Malakah Atarah

I never thought I could fast for 33 days. Thanks to the strong leadership and consistent support and availability from Chef Tawah Lightfoot El I was fasting and not... dying lol like I thought I would! I learned that 80% of the time I ate, it was out of boredom and not actual hunger. I then learned that 20% of my "hunger" was only my body asking for water, 10% of that time! We do not need to eat as much as we do! I refuse to overeat now. I feel like I had gastric bypass surgery and cannot mentally accept putting those large/excessive/unnecessary/empty calories/low nutrient foods into my body again. I want to know more about what my body actually NEEDS to operate. Chef Tawah's meals were a welcomed and delicious answer to that question. In the last 10 days of the fast he introduced us to his soup recipes that were amazingly nutritious and tastier than I ever imagined. They were also very easy to make. I am forever grateful to him for his encouragement and expertise in changing my mindset, relationship and approach to eating. I will fast 4 times a year as he recommends.

Sa-Auset:Tauwieret(C)(TM)

This class was truly amazing! Even though I didn't have a lot of time to chat with you guys because of work and school, this cleanse has truly helped me. I suffered from bad food allergies, IBS, and digestive disorder and every day I had discomfort and the sudden urge to rush to the restroom. Since I've been on this cleanse , I've not had one issue with any of these issues at all. I also suffered from hair loss and one day I went to wash my hair and noticed that my hair was not shedding and also my hair was growing back in the one spot it was broke off. On this cleanse I lost a total of 26 lbs and everyone at work is now calling me skinny! I was fatigue at first when starting the cleanse but now I am so full of energy. I was allergic to Brazil Nuts and during the cleanse I was able to use the Brazil nuts without having to rush to my emergency Epipen. I notice yeast leaving my body and not having an issue with that anymore. Once we were able to eat the beans I noticed that I'm not able to eat a lot which is a good thing! My issues with fibroids

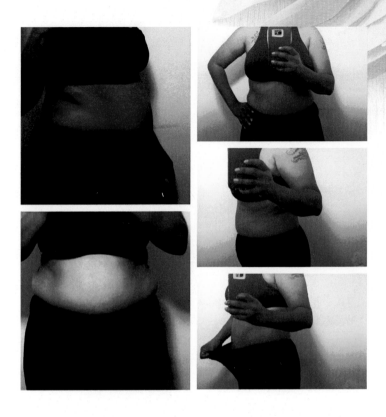

are gone! I stopped taking all of my meds for digestive issues and my allergy, which I had to take daily. I won't pack on all the weight again I feel 100% better

Ivy Thomas

Bibliography

Attia, P. (2012). *Is Ketosis Dangerous?*. [online] Eatingacademy. com. Available at: http://eatingacademy.com/nutrition /is-ketosis-dangerous [Accessed 28 Sep. 2017].

Bio.classes.ucsc.edu. (2012). *17 Osmoregulation II* . [online] Available at: http://bio.classes.ucsc.edu/bio131 /Thometz%20Website/ [Accessed 29 Sep. 2017].

Biotechnologyforums.com. (2017). *The Pathway Of Toxins In The Body – Entry To Elimination*. [online] Available at: https://www.biotechnologyforums.com /thread-1876.html [Accessed 28 Sep. 2017].

Campbell, A. (2017). *Ketones: Clearing Up the Confusion - Diabetes Self-Management*. [online] Diabetes Self-Management. Available at: https://www .diabetesselfmanagement.com/blog/ketones-clearing- up-the-confusion/ [Accessed 28 Sep. 2017].

Cancer.org. (n.d.). *What Is Non-Small Cell Lung Cancer?* [online] Available at: https://www.cancer.org/cancer /non-small-cell-lung-cancer/about/what-is-non-small- cell-lung-cancer.html [Accessed 28 Sep. 2017].

Chemistry.elmhurst.edu. (2017). *Overview Metabolism*. [online] Available at: http://chemistry.elmhurst.edu/ vchembook/600glycolysis.html [Accessed 28 Sep. 2017].

Creighton, J. (2016).Venomous vs Poisonous: *What Is the Difference Between Venom, Poison, and Toxins?*. [online] Futurism. Available at: https://futurism.com/what-is-the-difference-between-venom-poison-and-toxins/ [Accessed 28 Sep. 2017].

Crosta, P. (2017). *Scurvy: Causes, Symptoms, And Treatment.* [online] Medical News Today. Available at: https://www.medicalnewstoday.com/articles/155758.php [Accessed 28 Sep. 2017].

Dietitians of Canada. (2013). *Functions and Food Sources of Common Vitamins.* [online] Available at: https://www.dietitians.ca/Your-Health/Nutrition-A-Z/Vitamins/Functions-and-Food-Sources-of-Common-Vitamins.aspx [Accessed 28 Sep. 2017].

Ehrlich, S. (2013). *Vitamin H (Biotin).* [online] University of Maryland Medical Center. Available at: http://www.umm.edu/health/medical/altmed/supplement/vitamin-h-biotin [Accessed 28 Sep. 2017].

Ehrlich, S. (2016). *Vitamin E.* [online] University of Maryland Medical Center. Available at: http://www.umm.edu/health/medical/altmed/supplement/vitamin-e [Accessed 28 Sep. 2017].

En.wikipedia.org. (n.d.). *Fat.* [online] Available at: https://en.wikipedia.org/wiki/Fat [Accessed 28 Sep. 2017].

En.wikipedia.org. (n.d.). *Protein.* [online] Available at: https://en.wikipedia.org/wiki/Protein [Accessed 28 Sep. 2017].

Gilbert, S. (n.d.). *Kidney Structure and the Nephron.* [ebook] pp.1-12. Available at: http://ocw.tufts.edu/data/33/498083.pdf [Accessed 29 Sep. 2017].

Gill, R. (2016). *Riboflavin Deficiency: Overview, Riboflavin Requirements, Clinical Features of Deficiency (Ariboflavinosis).*

[online] Emedicine.medscape.com. Available at: http://emedicine.medscape.com/article/125193-overview#a3 [Accessed 28 Sep. 2017].

Health Freedom Resources. (n.d.). *Part 2: Symptoms of Liver Problems.* [online] Available at: https://healthfree.com/liver-problems-symptoms-2.html [Accessed 28 Sep. 2017].

Healthline. (n.d.). *Folate Deficiency.* [online] Available at: https://www.healthline.com/health/folate-deficiency#overview1 [Accessed 28 Sep. 2017].

Healthline. (n.d.). *Hartnup Disease.* [online] Available at: https://www.healthline.com/health/hartnup-disorder#overview1 [Accessed 28 Sep. 2017].

Healthline. (n.d.). *Hypercalcemia: What Happens If You Have Too Much Calcium?.* [online] Available at: https://www.healthline.com/health/hypercalcemia#symptoms2 [Accessed 28 Sep. 2017].

Healthline. (n.d.). *Rickets.* [online] Available at: https://www.healthline.com/health/rickets#risk-factors2 [Accessed 28 Sep. 2017].

Healthline. (n.d.). *Rickets.* [online] Available at: https://www.healthline.com/health/rickets#symptoms3 [Accessed 28 Sep. 2017].

Healthline. (n.d.). *The Symptoms of Vitamin B Deficiency.* [online] Available at: https://www.healthline.com/health/symptoms-of-vitamin-b-deficiency#vitamin-b6 [Accessed 28 Sep. 2017].

Healthline. (n.d.). *Wernicke-Korsakoff Syndrome.* [online] Available at: https://www.healthline.com/health/

wernicke-korsakoff-syndrome#overview1 [Accessed 28 Sep. 2017].

Home Reference. (2017). *What Are Proteins And What Do They Do?*. [online] Available at: https://ghr.nlm.nih.gov/primer/howgeneswork/protein [Accessed 28 Sep. 2017].

Inactivation and Detoxification of Xenobiotics and Metabolites in the Liver. (2012). [ebook] pp.1–8. Available at: http://www.comed.uobaghdad.edu.iq/uploads/Lectures/Biochemistry/biochemistry%2020122013/dr.%20hadaf/4Detoxification%20in%20the%20Liver2012.pdf [Accessed 29 Sep. 2017].

Keith on Food. (2011). *Detox Pathway: How To Detox Your Five Essential Organs*. [online] Available at: https://keithonfood.com/2011/08/03/live-longer-looking-younger/ [Accessed 28 Sep. 2017].

Li, S., Tan, H., Wang, N., Zhang, Z., Lao, L., Wong, C. and Feng, Y. (2017). *The Role of Oxidative Stress and Antioxidants in Liver Diseases*. [online] NCBI. Available at: https://www.ncbi.nlm.nih.gov/pmc/articles/PMC4661801/ [Accessed 28 Sep. 2017].

Lobo, V., Patil, A., Phatak, A. and Chandra, N. (2010). *Free Radicals, Antioxidants And Functional Foods: Impact On Human Health*. [online] NCBI. Available at: https://www.ncbi.nlm.nih.gov/pmc/articles/PMC3249911/ [Accessed 28 Sep. 2017].

Lymphcareusa.com. (n.d.). *Lymphatic System*. [online] Available at: https://www.lymphcareusa.com/patient/lymph–a–what/what–is–lymphedema/lymphatic-system.html [Accessed 28 Sep. 2017].

Mader, S.S.(1997). *Inquiry Into Life*. Boston: WCB MCGraw-Hill.

Nat5biopl.edubuzz.org. (n.d.). *5. Proteins & Enzymes - National 5 Biology*. [online] Available at: http://nat5biopl.edubuzz.org/unit-1-cell-biology/5-proteins-enzymes [Accessed 28 Sep. 2017].

National Institute of Diabetes and Digestive and Kidney Diseases. (2013). *The Digestive System & How it Works* | NIDDK. [online] Available at: https://www.niddk.nih.gov/health-information/digestive-diseases/digestive-system-how-it-works [Accessed 28 Sep. 2017].

Peluso, M. (n.d.). What Are the Products *When Carbohydrates and Fats Are Metabolized?*. [online] Healthyeating.sfgate.com. Available at: http://healthyeating.sfgate.com/products-carbohydrates-fats-metabolized-5772.html [Accessed 28 Sep. 2017].

Pham-Huy, C. and Pham-Huy, L. (2008). *Free Radicals, Antioxidants in Disease and Health*. [online] PubMed Central (PMC). Available at: https://www.ncbi.nlm.nih.gov/pmc/articles/PMC3614697/ [Accessed 28 Sep. 2017].

Reference, G. (2017). *What Are Proteins And What Do They Do?*. [online] Genetics Home Reference. Available at: https://ghr.nlm.nih.gov/primer/howgeneswork/protein [Accessed 28 Sep. 2017].

Rosenbloom, M. (2016). *Vitamin Toxicity Clinical Presentation: History, Physical Examination*. [online] Emedicine.medscape.com. Available at: http://emedicine.medscape.com/article/819426-clinical [Accessed 28 Sep. 2017].

Szalay, J. (2017). *What Are Carbohydrates?*. [online]
Live Science. Available at: https://www.livescience.
com/51976-carbohydrates.html [Accessed 28 Sep. 2017].

The National Kidney Foundation. (n.d.). *How Your Kidneys
Work*. [online] Available at: https://www.kidney.org/
kidneydisease/howkidneyswrk [Accessed 28 Sep. 2017].

Vivo.colostate.edu. (2017). *Metabolic Functions of the
Liver*. [online] Available at: http://www.vivo.colostate.
edu/hbooks/pathphys/digestion/liver/metabolic.html
[Accessed 28 Sep. 2017].

WebMD. (2017). *Symptoms of Depression*. [online]
Available at: http://www.webmd.com/depression/
guide/detecting-depression#1 [Accessed 28 Sep. 2017].

WebMD. (2017). *Vitamin B12 Deficiency: Causes,
Symptoms, and Treatment*. [online] Available at: http://
www.webmd.com/diet/vitamin-b12-deficiency-
symptoms-causes#2 [Accessed 28 Sep. 2017].

Webmd.com. (n.d.). *PANTOTHENIC ACID VITAMIN B5:
Uses, Side Effects, Interactions And Warnings*. [online] Available
at: http://www.webmd.com/vitamins-supplements/
ingredientmono-853-PANTOTHENIC+ACID
+VITAMIN+B5.aspx [Accessed 28 Sep. 2017].

Wilcox-O'Hearn, L. (2012). *Myths*. [online] Ketotic.
org. Available at: http://www.ketotic.org/p/myths.html
[Accessed 28 Sep. 2017].

Zeratsky, K. (2015). *How Much Vitamin C Is Too Much?*.
[online] Mayo Clinic. Available at: http://www.
mayoclinic.org/healthy-lifestyle/nutrition-and-healthy-
eating/expert-answers/vitamin-c/faq-20058030

[Accessed 28 Sep. 2017].

Zeratsky, K. (2017). *Niacin overdose: What are the symptoms?*. [online] Mayo Clinic. Available at: http://www.mayoclinic.org /diseases-conditions/high-blood-cholesterol/expert-answers/niacin-overdose/faq-20058075 [Accessed 28 Sep. 2017].

INDEX

K

Kidneys, *13*

L

Lungs, *15*

M

Magnesium, *32*

Meditation, *42*

N

Navy Bean Soup, 72

Night Blindness, *30*

Nutrients, *18*

Nutrition, *18*

Nutritional Anti-Oxidants, *38*

O

Office Toxins, 7

Organs Responsible For Detoxification, *10*

oxidative stress, *36*

Oxidative stress, *36*

P

Pancreatic beta cells, *35*

R

Reactive Nitrogenous Species, *36*

Reactive Oxidative Species, *36*

Ribose, 19

Rickets, *31*

RNS. *See* Reactive Nitrogenous Species

ROS, 36

S

Salt Water Flush, *47*

Saturated Fat, *25*

Scurvy, *31*

Second Approach, *8*

Selenium, *32*, *40*

Serine, *22*

Signs and Symptoms of Toxicity, *4*

Skin, *17*

Sodium, *33*

Source of antioxidants, *37*

Stairmaster, *63*

Made in the USA
Lexington, KY
01 March 2018